cooking forkids

cookingforkids

Anna West

Published by SILVERDALE BOOKS
An imprint of Bookmart Ltd
Registered number 2372865
Trading as Bookmart Ltd
Blaby Road
Wigston
Leicester LE18 4SE

© 2007 D&S Books Ltd

D&S Books Ltd
Kerswell,
Parkham Ash, Bideford
Devon, England
EX39 5PR

e-mail us at:-
enquiries@d-sbooks.co.uk

This edition printed 2007

ISBN -10: 1-84509-461-1
ISBN -13: 9-781-84509-461-4

DS0163. Cooking for kids

Creative director: Sarah King
Editor: Anna Southgate
Project editor: Clare Haworth-Maden
Designer: Debbie Fisher
Photographer: Paul Stewart-Reed

Fonts: Vag Rounded and Badger

Printed in Thailand

1 3 5 7 9 10 8 6 4 2

contents

introduction
for parents

One of the best ways to teach children about healthy eating is to involve them in cooking for themselves, their family and friends. The ability to plan a menu, go shopping for ingredients and prepare food gives children a huge sense of pride and achievement, while teaching an important life skill.

This book is aimed at 8–12-year-olds, although most recipes are suitable for younger children with adult supervision and help. Supervision may involve handling knives, an oven or electrical equipment, and will depend on the age and skill of the child.

Encourage children to choose simple recipes to make at the beginning and gradually build up their confidence to create an entire meal. Help them to choose contrasting colours, flavours and textures, and to create a well-balanced meal, using ingredients from the main food groups (see page 8).

Involve children in shopping for ingredients so they can learn about label-reading and choosing the best and freshest ingredients. Get them to hand over money to pay for food and help with the packing and unpacking of shopping. Encourage children to think about where the food they eat comes from, where it grows, is reared or produced.

There is a wide range of recipes to choose from, including breakfasts, snacks and main meals, as well as a few sweet treats. There are also chapters for those with special diets and vegetarians. I hope your children will enjoy cooking and eating delicious food, and will form habits that will last them a lifetime.

introduction
for children

This book has many recipes that are delicious, nutritious and fun to make. Each recipe tells you the following:

Please take time to read through this helpful information and the pages about safety and what to do before you start cooking. It may seem boring, but the information is there to make your cooking a success and to keep you safe and healthy. You may need some adult help with using the oven or tricky techniques – just make sure you take all the credit, though!

Have fun making your food look and taste fantastic!

- How many people it will serve
- Preparation (making) time
- Cooking time
- Oven temperature
- Cooking utensils needed
- List of ingredients
- Step-by-step instructions with photos of children showing you what to do
- Recipe ideas for serving or using alternative ingredients

a healthy diet

Your diet affects how you feel, as well as your growth and development. We are what we eat, so we must ensure we eat the correct food to give us energy and all the nutrients we need. Eating 5 portions (or more) of fruit and vegetables a day can help keep you healthier by helping protect against some cancers, obesity, coronary heart disease and type 2 diabetes.

1 Fruit and vegetables: 33% of the plate; eat 5+ portions a day; e.g., fresh, frozen, canned, dried or juice of fruit

2 Bread, potatoes and other cereals: 33% of the plate; eat 5 portions a day; e.g., pasta, rice, noodles, crackers, potatoes, bread, breakfast cereal

3 Meat, fish and alternatives: 12% of the plate; eat 2–3 portions a day; e.g., beef, lamb, salmon, mackerel, sardines, eggs, beans and lentils, nuts

4 Milk and dairy: 15% of the plate; eat 3 portions a day; e.g., milkshakes, milk, yogurt, fromage frais, hard and soft cheese

5 Fatty and sugary foods: 7% of the plate; eat in moderation, depending on how active you are; e.g., crisps, butter, spreads, cream, sauces, sugar, jam, biscuits, sweets, chocolate, processed food, fizzy dinks, deep-fried food

what do we need food for?

- We need fluid every day to keep us hydrated and full of energy, and to help our brain concentrate. Drink 6–8 glasses a day. Try to avoid sugary drinks, but drink water throughout the day, and fruit juice or milk at mealtimes.

- For energy, so we can work and play, we need carbohydrates and limited fatty/sugary foods: wholemeal bread, cereals, potatoes, wholemeal pasta and rice, limited amounts of cakes, butter, cream and crisps.

- For growth and repair of muscles, skin, nails, bones, blood, organs, nerves and the brain, we need protein, found in meat, fish and alternatives, e.g., peas, eggs, baked beans and nuts.

- For keeping a healthy gut and digestive system, we need fibre, found in wholemeal and wholegrain porridge, pasta and bread, fruit and vegetables.

- For keeping you healthy and making you look healthy, we need vitamins and minerals, found in milk and dairy foods, green leafy vegetables, red meat, fish, breakfast cereals, dried fruit, beans, nuts, seeds, coloured fruit and vegetables, cheese and eggs.

- Salt: a little salt helps keep the correct amount of fluid in the body. Use a little to help flavours during cooking if a recipe requires it, but leave the salt pot off the table, as too much can cause heart problems.

Some foods can help provide food from more than one food group, for example: ham and pineapple pizza.

Base = bread group

Tomato topping = fruit and vegetable group

Pineapple = fruit and vegetable group

Ham = meat and fish group

Cheese = milk and dairy group

getting ready

1 Do not cook if you are feeling unwell.

2 Remove pets from the kitchen area.

3 Wear a clean apron and roll up long sleeves.

4 Tie back long hair.

5 Wash your hands with warm soapy water and then dry thoroughly on a clean towel.

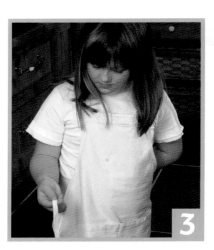

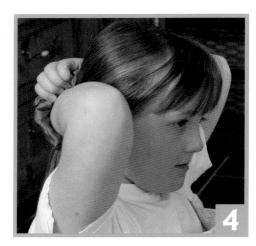

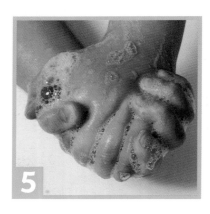

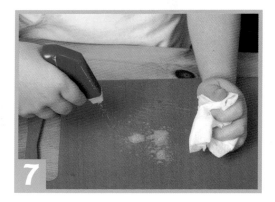

6 Cover any cuts or sores with a plaster (blue plasters are best as they can be easily spotted in food if they fall off).

7 Clear the work surface you want to use and clean with hot soapy water or antibacterial spray and a clean cloth.

8 Read the recipe right through.

9 Assemble your tools and ingredients.

10 Wash fruit and vegetables before cooking to remove dirt and any chemicals.

11 Turn the oven on to the correct temperature if necessary.

during cooking

1 Each recipe gives both metric and imperial weights. Keep to one set of measurements or the other. 'A spoonful' means 1 level spoonful unless otherwise stated.

2 Do not lick your fingers or equipment during cooking.

3 Taste your food as you go along to know how thing are working out. Use a clean spoon and always wash it afterwards.

4 Take your time, don't rush and take care when using equipment.

5 (Above) Make sure pan handles do not point outwards because they could easily be knocked and cause an accident. Handles should always point away from you.

6 Use chopping boards to cut food on. Raw meat should be cut on a separate board, which should be scrubbed thoroughly afterwards with hot soapy water.

7 Take care when using sharp knives. Learn the cookery claw (see page 12).

8 Use clean dishcloths, tea towels and hand towels.

9 Clean up any mess or spills straightaway from the work surface or floor.

10 Use oven gloves when using the oven.

11 Don't leave metal spoons in saucepans on the hob – they get hot!

12 Lay knives flat on the work surface when they are not in use.

13 Beware of steam when opening the oven door and taking lids off saucepans.

14 If you do burn yourself, put the affected part under cold water for 10 minutes and get adult help.

15 If a pan catches fire, cover it with a damp tea towel and get adult help.

knife safety

1 Do not use blunt knives – they are more dangerous than sharp ones.

2 Do not leave knives in the sink where they cannot be seen, especially under water.

3 Use the correct knife for the job – a small knife for preparing fruit and vegetables; a medium knife for chopping and slicing.

4 If a knife has to be carried, ensure the point is kept towards the floor and the sharp edge is facing backwards.

5 Place knives flat on the work surface.

The cookery claw

1 Use the hand you feel most comfortable with to hold a knife handle. Place it between your thumb and index finger; grip your fingers around the handle.

2 With your other hand, place your fingertips in a straight line, near to the edge of the food you wish to cut.

3 Make sure your fingertips are parallel to the knife blade to avoid cutting yourself. Tuck your thumb behind your fingers with your nails slanting inwards

4 Carefully slice the food just in front of your fingertips and slide your hand backwards in small steps after each cut.

food safety

1 Defrost frozen food completely before use.

2 Check use-by and best-before dates on food; throw away anything that exceeds the dates.

3 Store raw and cooked food separately in the fridge. Raw food should be kept at the bottom of the fridge so it doesn't drip onto any food below it.

4 Make sure the fridge temperature is kept between 0–5ºC (32–41ºF).

5 Always wash your hands before cooking, and after using the toilet, sneezing, blowing your nose, coughing or touching your face, the bin or animals.

6 Keep the kitchen clean and tidy.

7 Avoid eating raw egg.

8 Check to make sure food is cooked correctly, especially chicken or pork. If food is reheated, ensure it is really piping hot right through. Never reheat food more than once.

9 Do not use food from damaged tins/packets.

after cooking

1 Check you have turned off all gas and electrical equipment.

2 Tidy away remaining ingredients.

3 Put rubbish in the bin.

4 Wash up.

5 Freeze or save any cooled leftovers – make sure they are covered with a lid, plastic wrap or foil.

6 Remove your apron and wash your hands.

hints & tips

- Get to know the equipment you are using, especially the oven. Is it a fan oven? If so, reduce the temperature by 20°C (68°F). If your oven is too cold, adjust the temperature upwards.

- Try growing your own fresh herbs to experiment with flavouring and garnishing your food.

- Experiment with food flavours and create your own dishes.

- Use a kitchen timer (make sure it's loud) to ensure food is cooked to perfection and not overdone. It is also handy to use if cooking more than one dish at a time.

- Take eggs out of the fridge for a while before cooking, to get them to room temperature. To whisk egg whites, make sure the utensils and bowl are grease free and that no egg yolk gets into the bowl.

utensils

Here are all the utensils you will need for the recipes in this book:

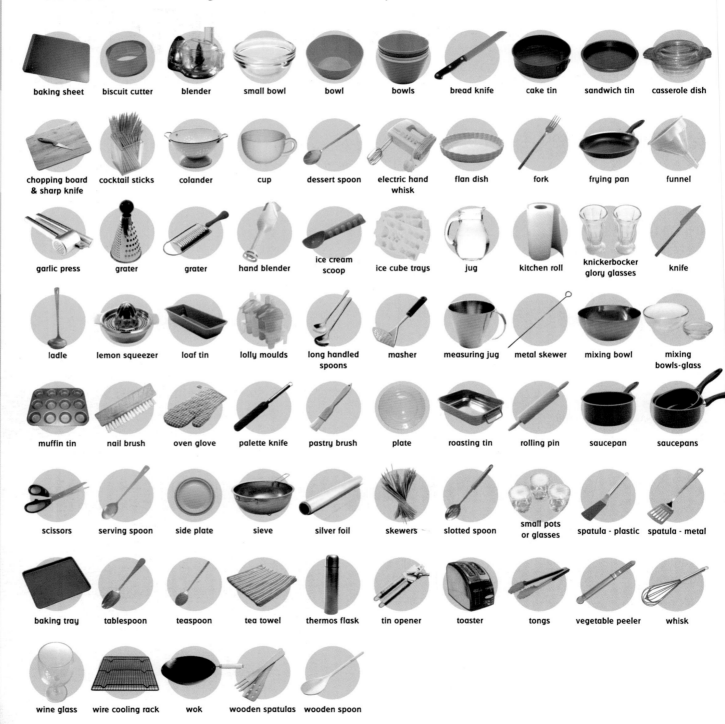

baking sheet | biscuit cutter | blender | small bowl | bowl | bowls | bread knife | cake tin | sandwich tin | casserole dish

chopping board & sharp knife | cocktail sticks | colander | cup | dessert spoon | electric hand whisk | flan dish | fork | frying pan | funnel

garlic press | grater | grater | hand blender | ice cream scoop | ice cube trays | jug | kitchen roll | knickerbocker glory glasses | knife

ladle | lemon squeezer | loaf tin | lolly moulds | long handled spoons | masher | measuring jug | metal skewer | mixing bowl | mixing bowls-glass

muffin tin | nail brush | oven glove | palette knife | pastry brush | plate | roasting tin | rolling pin | saucepan | saucepans

scissors | serving spoon | side plate | sieve | silver foil | skewers | slotted spoon | small pots or glasses | spatula - plastic | spatula - metal

baking tray | tablespoon | teaspoon | tea towel | thermos flask | tin opener | toaster | tongs | vegetable peeler | whisk

wine glass | wire cooling rack | wok | wooden spatulas | wooden spoon

cooking methods and techniques

Here are explanations and instructions for the various food preparation and cooking techniques used in the recipes.

Baking
This is cooking in an oven.

Basting

This prevents food from drying out during cooking, adds flavour and improves the appearance of food.

1 Use oven gloves to remove the dish from the oven and place on a trivet.

2 Spoon juices/liquid/sauce over the meat/vegetables until well covered.

3 Return the dish to the oven and repeat as necessary.

Boiling
Boiling is cooking liquid at 100°C (212°F). Bubbles rise to the surface of the water and the surface of the water moves rapidly.

Simmering
This means to keep a liquid just below boiling point. Bring the liquid to the boil first, then reduce the temperature until the surface of the liquid is just moving.

Frying
This is cooking food in fat or oil.

Stir-frying

This is a method of cooking food quickly in hot oil in a wok or large frying pan. The oil is heated until smoky hot and the food is constantly stirred during cooking. Stir-frying is a healthy way of cooking as vegetables are cooked until just tender, so few vitamins are lost.

Testing oil is hot

1 Add required oil to the pan you are using and turn heat on. Drop a small cube of bread into the oil.

2 When it starts to sizzle and turn brown, the oil is hot.

Remove bread with a slotted spoon and start cooking immediately.

Grilling

To cook under a grill or over a naked flame. The food is cooked on a rack in a grill pan so that fat can escape into the pan. Food must be turned during cooking with tongs or a fork.

Checking meat is cooked

For safest results, use a meat thermometer. Put it into the thickest part of the meat, away from any bones. The temperature should reach 80°C (175°F) for well-cooked meat. Alternatively, insert a skewer or knife into the thickest part of the meat. Make sure the juices run out clear. Pink or red juices mean the meat requires extra cooking. Be extra careful when cooking chicken or pork as these must be cooked thoroughly to avoid food poisoning.

Peeling and chopping an onion

1 Cut a small slice from the top of an onion.

2 Peel off the skin with your fingers.

3 To chop, cut the onion in half lengthways.

4 Place the onion flat side down onto the chopping board and make approximately five cuts horizontally towards the root, but not right through.

5 Now repeat, but cut vertically.

6 Slice the onion across at even intervals to create even-sized chopped-onion pieces. Repeat with the other half.

For rings, cut the onion crossways into slices and separate into rings.

Cutting vegetables

1 Peel vegetable with a vegetable peeler/knife, if required. Baby vegetables can simply be scrubbed clean with a clean nail brush in water

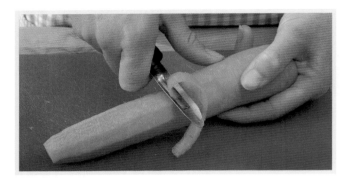

2 Trim off stalk and bottom of vegetable.

3 For slices, cut 3 mm (¹/₈ in) slices; for batons, trim each slice to make a square shape and cut into 3 mm (¹/₈ in) strips; to dice, cut each baton crossways into 3 mm (¹/₈ in) pieces.

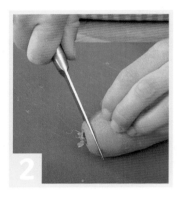

For broccoli, cut florets from head.

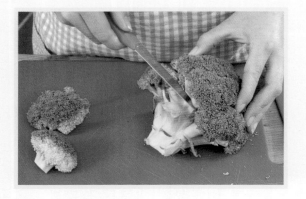

Deseeding peppers

1 Rinse the pepper in clean water and dry on kitchen paper. Cut a thin slice to remove the stem and base. Cut a slice horizontally through one side of the pepper.

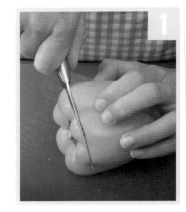

2 Open the pepper out flat.

3 Remove the seeds and membrane using your fingers or a knife. Discard the insides.

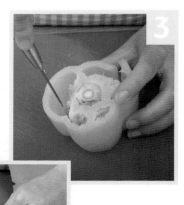

4 Cut into thin slices or dice.

To make rings, omit step 2.

Salting an aubergine

This removes bitter juices and reduces the amount of oil absorbed during cooking.

1 Cut off the stem and trim a slice from the end. Slice the aubergine into the size required for the recipe. With large aubergines, you may need to cut the aubergine in half first.

2 Place the sliced aubergine in a dish. Sprinkle salt over the layers of aubergine and leave for 30–45 minutes.

3 Gently squeeze excess moisture from the sliced aubergine.

4 Rinse under clean water and dry on kitchen paper.

Crushing garlic

1 Cut a very thin slice to remove the root from the clove of garlic.

2 Peel off the outer papery skin.

3 Place in a garlic crusher and squeeze the handles together over a chopping board/small plate.

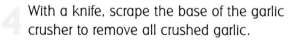

4 With a knife, scrape the base of the garlic crusher to remove all crushed garlic.

Grating cheese, carrots and citrus fruit

The edges of graters are sharp, so that when food is rubbed across them they shave off threads of food. Graters have different-sized holes, and, as a rough guide, the large holes are used for cheese and vegetables, while the small holes are used for citrus fruits or Parmesan cheese.

1 Hold the food approximately 1 cm (½ in) from its edge by your fingertips.

2 Ensure the ends of your fingers are bent parallel to the grater and not lying flat along the food.

3 Curl your nails inwards and carefully watch what you are doing.

4 Slowly move your hand up and down the length of the grater until the food is grated. When your fingers get near to the grater, move your grip back at 1 cm (½ in) intervals and continue grating.

Checking vegetables are cooked

Use a sharp knife. Carefully remove one piece of vegetable after the recommended cooking time. Use the tip of a sharp knife or skewer and see if it slides in easily. If the vegetable still feels hard, cook for a few minutes more before testing again.

Juicing citrus fruits

1 Cut the fruit in half.

2 Place the cut side of the fruit onto the centre of a lemon-squeezer.

3 Push the fruit down with your hand and squish from side to side to remove the juice.

Preparing a mango

1 Cut off the ends.

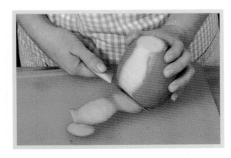

2 Thinly remove the mango skin using a sharp knife or a vegetable peeler.

3 Cut a large slice from one side of the fruit, cutting close to the stone. Cut another slice from the opposite side, close to the stone. Cut the remaining flesh from the stone.

4 Cut into slices or chunks.

Note: Do not eat mango skin.

Coring an apple

1 Holding the apple firmly in one hand, hold an apple-corer in the other hand at a 45° angle. Peel around the apple to remove the skin.

2 Use the tip of the corer to remove the core by pushing down the side of the core and cutting around it.

3 Remove the apple core by gently pulling on the stalk.

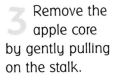

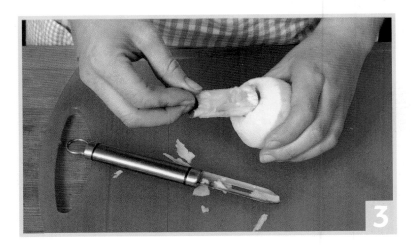

Removing an avocado stone

1 Cut around the fruit lengthways, right through to the stone.

2 Twist the two halves in opposite directions until they come apart or use the side of a knife.

3 Open the halves.

4 Remove the stone with a spoon or the point of a sharp knife.

5 To peel, use a vegetable peeler.

After preparation, avocados should be brushed with lemon juice to prevent the flesh turning brown.

Prepare chilli peppers

Rubber or plastic gloves can be worn while preparing chilli peppers.

1 Cut a thin slice to remove the stalk.

2 Remove the end.

3 Cut in half lengthways.

4 Open out.

5 Remove seeds with a sharp knife for a less hot flavour. Thinly slice and chop chilli.

6 Always wash your hands after touching a chilli, and avoid any contact with your eyes.

Separating eggs

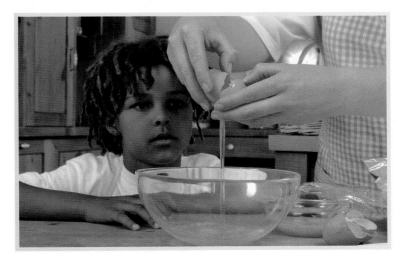

1 Get two cups or small bowls. Tap the egg once, sharply, on the side of a cup/bowl to crack the shell. Gently place your thumbnails just inside the crack to pull the shell apart.

2 Turn your hands so that the inside of the egg is facing you. Make sure the yolk is kept in one piece and is in one half of the shell. Let the egg white slide into the cup below.

3 Slide the yolk from one half of shell to the other, until all the egg white has fallen away. Slide the yolk into a separate cup.

Boiling eggs

1 Place eggs in a saucepan and cover with cold water.

2 Bring to the boil and simmer for 3 minutes for a runny yolk. Remove from saucepan with a slotted spoon.

3 Simmer eggs for 10 minutes for a hard yolk. Drain away hot water and run cold water over the eggs for 1–2 minutes. Tap the egg shells and leave to cool before peeling off the shells.

Poaching eggs

1 Add 5 cm (2 in) water to a saucepan with a pinch of salt or dash of vinegar.

2 When the water is simmering, swirl the water with a spoon and slide the egg (remove the shell first) into the water.

3 Cook until set, approximately 2 minutes for a runny yolk. Remove egg from pan with a slotted spoon.

Making breadcrumbs

Use bread that is a few days old for making breadcrumbs.

1 Break the bread into pieces and put into a food processor/blender.

2 Whizz until crumbed (crumb a few slices at a time for best results).

Alternatively, use a wire sieve or grater.

Sifting

A sieve is used to add air to the mixture and remove lumps from ingredients like flour. Put the ingredient to be sieved up to half full in the sieve and gently tap on your hand over a bowl.

Beating

This is mixing hard with a spoon, fork, whisk or electric mixer.

Creaming

Used in cake-making, this is beating together fat and sugar until the mix is pale and fluffy.

Folding in

Use this method to combine ingredients and to keep the mixture light. It is important not to be rough with the mixture or all the air will be knocked out of the mix, which will result in a flat, failed recipe

1 Use a metal spoon to cut through the centre of the mix and turn over that section of mixture.

2 Give the bowl a quarter-turn and repeat until the mixture is just combined.

Whipping/whisking

Use a hand or electric whisk to beat air into a food such as egg white or cream until it is stiff. When the whisk is removed, the food should create peaks that stick up and stay there. Be careful not to over-whisk/whip foods as they will be ruined.

Rubbing in

This method is used when making pastry, cakes, scones and biscuits.

1 'Work' the fat into the flour by rubbing it between your fingertips and thumbs until the mixture resembles fine breadcrumbs.

2 Make sure all the fat is rubbed into the flour, but do not over-rub the mixture.

3 Keep your hands above the bowl and avoid using the palms of your hands.

Kneading dough

This combines the dough mixture evenly and makes it more pliable and edible. A food mixer can be used or it can be done by hand. Shape the dough into a ball on a floury work surface. Lightly knead dough for pastry or scones using fingertips only. Bring the edges of the dough into the centre, turn dough over and repeat until ingredients are combined.

For pizza dough, you can shape it using your hands, but this is quite tricky!

Bread or pasta dough needs stronger kneading

1 Pull out the end of the dough with your hand.

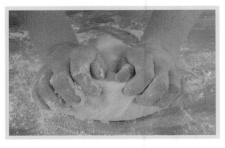

2 Fold the dough inwards.

3 Push it with the heel of your hand to stretch the dough. Give the dough a quarter-turn and repeat until kneaded for the required amount of time.

Greasing a tin or dish

Rub with butter, oil or lard to prevent food sticking to it.

Greasing and lining a baking tray

1 Lay the tin down on greaseproof or non-stick paper, and draw around it with a pencil.

2 Lay the tin on its side and mark out the top and base of the tin. Roll the tin along the paper to measure the length needed to go around the tin.

3 Cut out the shapes from the paper.

4 Brush or rub the inside of the tin with melted butter or oil.

5 Lay the paper inside the tin and then regrease with more oil or melted butter.

Checking cake consistency

Use a metal spoon to pick up a spoonful of mixture. Hold the spoon above the mixing bowl and time (or count) three seconds. The mixture should drop on the count of three.

If it doesn't, the mixture is too stiff, so add a little milk. If the mixture falls quicker, it is too runny, so add a little sifted flour until you have the correct consistency.

To check a cake is cooked

Cakes should be well risen, golden brown and starting to shrink away from the edges of the tin. When you touch the centre, it should be firm. After the correct amount of cooking time:

1 Press the centre of the cake lightly with a fingertip. It should be springy and no fingertip marks should be left.

2 Put a long skewer into the middle of the cake and remove. Make sure there isn't any gooey mixture stuck to it.

3 If the cake shows signs of being undercooked, return it to the oven for a further 5 minutes' cooking time and then check again.

cooked   *needs more cooking*

Rolling out and lining a dish with pastry

Grease the dish to be lined with margarine.

1 Sprinkle flour on both work surface and rolling pin. Roll pastry out in one direction, using even pressure on the rolling pin.

2 Give the pastry a quarter-turn. Reroll and continue steps 2 and 3 until pastry is 3 mm (⅛ in) thick and is larger than the dish to be lined (remember, the pastry has to line the sides of the dish, too).

3 Lay the rolling pin halfway across the pastry and pick up the bottom edge of the pastry. Gently pull the pastry on top of the rolling pin and hold just above the dish to be lined.

4 Slide the rolled pastry from the rolling pin into the dish and gently pat into the contours of the dish.

5 Use a sharp knife to trim the edges of the pastry flat and even to the dish edge.

It is best to leave the pastry to 'rest' in the dish for 30 minutes to prevent it shrinking when cooked, so cover with plastic wrap and put it in the fridge. After 30 minutes, remove from the fridge and remove the plastic wrap. Continue with your recipe.

Seasoning

This is when you add salt, pepper, spices or herbs to your cooking to improve the flavour. Check to see if the seasoning needs adjusting at the end of cooking your recipe.

Marinating

This is a way of making some food, such as meat or fish, more tender, and giving it extra flavour and moisture. Food should marinate for at least an hour or, preferably, overnight.

Glazing

This is how to finish off food with a glossy coating. Some foods are glazed with egg, butter, milk or syrup before cooking to make them go brown. Vegetables can be glazed with butter or sugar before or after cooking. Some foods can be glazed with a syrup or jelly. Use a pastry brush or the back of a spoon – whichever you find easiest.

garnishes

Sometimes when you're preparing food for special occasions, you might want to add some special touches. Here are a few ideas for garnishes.

carrot flowers

ingredients

1 medium carrot

15 cm (6 in) cucumber

Few chives

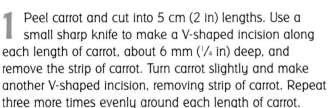

1 Peel carrot and cut into 5 cm (2 in) lengths. Use a small sharp knife to make a V-shaped incision along each length of carrot, about 6 mm (¼ in) deep, and remove the strip of carrot. Turn carrot slightly and make another V-shaped incision, removing strip of carrot. Repeat three more times evenly around each length of carrot.

2 Cut carrot into 6 mm (¼ in) slices, place on serving plate and use chive stems to resemble stalks.

3 For leaves, cut a long strip of cucumber skin and cut diagonally across the strip at 1 cm (½ in) intervals.

vegetable bundles

ingredients

1 spring onion

1 medium carrot

1 Trim top and bottom from carrot, peel and cut into 5 cm (2 in) lengths. Lay a piece on a chopping board and cut rounded edges off lengthwise to make a rectangular shape. Repeat with each chunk.

2 Cut each rectangle lengthwise into 3 mm ($\frac{1}{8}$ in) slices. Cut each sheet into 3 mm ($\frac{1}{8}$ in) matchsticks.

3 Cut green part from spring onion and put into a colander. Pour over hot water to soften the leaves. Rinse in cold water and pat dry with kitchen roll.

4 Cut spring-onion greens into long narrow strips (lengthwise) and use each strip to tie a bundle of carrot matchsticks together.

recipe tip
Use other vegetables, such as cooked potatoes, swedes, squashes or raw parsnips and peppers.

lemon pig

ingredients
1 lemon with pointy end
and 1 thin slice of lemon

2 cloves

1 The pointy end of the lemon will be the pig's nose, so use a cocktail stick to make a hole at each side of the nose for eyes and push a clove in each hole.

2 Cut a small wedge out underneath the pig's nose for a mouth. Make a hole at the opposite end where a tail would go. Use a knife to cut the ears.

3 From the slice of lemon, cut a strip of rind and push this in the tail hole.

4 Place 4 cocktail sticks underneath the lemon for legs. Stand the pig up to make sure it is balanced.

> **recipe tip**
> Use cubes of cheese and pineapple, baby cocktail onions or sausage chunks to decorate the pig.

now you are ready to start cooking!

Remember!

HOT things are dangerous

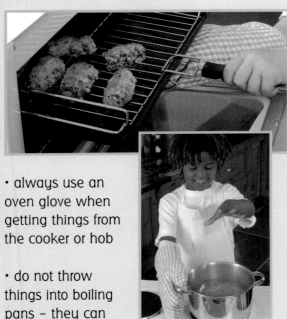

- always use an oven glove when getting things from the cooker or hob

- do not throw things into boiling pans – they can splash

- always make sure an adult is there to help

SHARP things are dangerous

- always make sure an adult is there to help

- remember how to use knives correctly

breakfasts

fruit faces

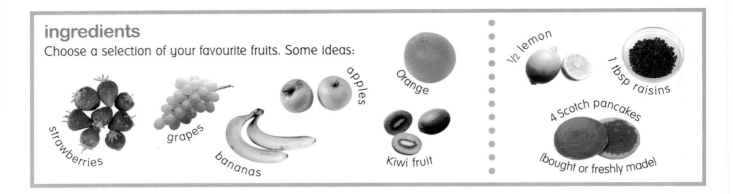

ingredients

Choose a selection of your favourite fruits. Some ideas:

strawberries · grapes · bananas · apples · Orange · Kiwi fruit · ½ lemon · 1 tbsp raisins · 4 Scotch pancakes (bought or freshly made)

1 Wash and dry all the fruit, except raisins and any fruit that needs skin removed (e.g., banana). Peel oranges and separate the segments.

2 Remove stalks from strawberries and thinly slice. Peel kiwi fruit and thinly slice. Cut grapes in half.

3 Peel apples, remove core and thinly slice. Add a squeeze of lemon juice to the bowl and mix.

4 Peel banana and slice. Add a squeeze of lemon juice to the bowl and mix gently.

recipe ideas
Arrange fruit straight onto a plate.
Try using rice cakes, toasted
muffins or crisp bread spread with
your favourite topping, such as
jam, soft cheese or honey.

5 Toast the Scotch pancakes until
warmed. Put onto a plate. Arrange
fruit on top of pancakes to make animal,
or funny, faces.

recipe tip
Adding lemon juice to
some cut fruit and
vegetables stops them
changing colour.

jam omelette

ingredients

1 tbsp oil or margarine

2 pinches caster sugar

2 eggs

1 tbsp warmed jam

1 Break the eggs into a small bowl and add a pinch of sugar.

2 Beat well with a fork until the whites and yolks are combined.

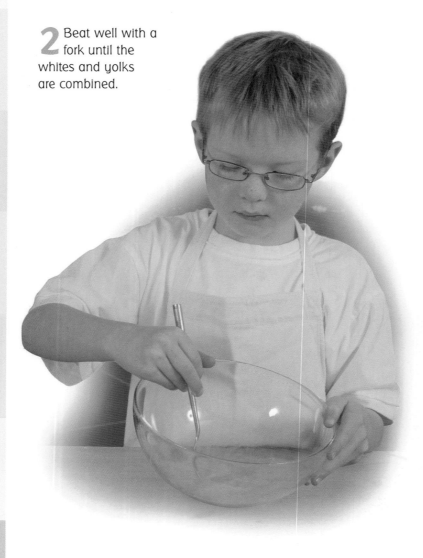

3 Heat the frying pan and add enough margarine or oil to cover the base lightly.

4 Pour the eggs into the pan and gently shake the pan while stirring the eggs, until the mixture is smooth and just going stiff.

5 Remove pan from heat and spoon jam into middle of egg mixture. Loosen the edge of omelette with the spatula.

6 Tilt the pan and fold omelette in half. Cook a little longer, then slide it onto a plate. Sprinkle with the remaining caster sugar.

recipe ideas
Add a pinch of salt and pepper to the mixture instead of sugar and add any of the following to the beaten egg at step 2: 25 g (1 oz) chopped ham, 1 dessertspoon grated Parmesan cheese, 25 g (1 oz) chopped tomatoes, 25 g (1 oz) tinned tuna or 25 g (1 oz) sliced mushrooms.

sunshine breakfast

1 Sift flour and salt into bowl. Add egg.

ingredients

100 g (4 oz) self-raising flour

150 ml (5 fl oz) milk

Pinch of salt

1 egg

2 tsp melted butter or margarine

25 g (1 oz) dried apricots

Oil for frying

25 g (1 oz) dried dates

2 Oranges

4 plain oat biscuits

2 tbsp jam

2 Pour in milk gradually, beating continually with a spoon to make a smooth batter.

3 Stir in melted butter. Chop the dried fruit into small chunks and stir into the batter.

4 Brush frying pan with oil and heat until hot. Spoon mixture into the frying pan to create small rounds.

5 Cook two rounds at a time for 1-2 minutes. Using a spatula, turn the rounds over and cook until brown on both sides. When cooked, keep fruity rounds warm by wrapping in a clean tea towel.

6 Peel oranges and separate the segments. Cut the oat biscuits into fingers and spread with jam, arrange on plate, with a fruity round in the centre, to look like the sun.

recipe ideas
Instead of adding dried fruit to mixture, try slices of fresh fruit or grated cheese. Spread oat biscuits with soft cheese.

recipe tip
Make the cooked rounds in bigger batches and freeze them. Once cool, layer them in a plastic tub with sheets of greaseproof paper. Just defrost and pop in the toaster to reheat. They are delicious served with a drizzle of maple syrup or golden syrup for a special treat.

fruity muesli

ingredients

75 g (3 oz) oats

25 g (1 oz) grapes

1 apple

15 g (½ oz) apricots

125 ml (4 fl oz) apple juice

15 g (½ oz) sultanas

50 g (2 oz) breakfast cereal (e.g., cornflakes)

300 ml (½ pt) milk, to serve

1 Put oats into mixing bowl and add apple juice. Soak for 30 minutes.

2 Wash grapes and cut in half. Add to mixing bowl.

3 Chop apricots into four pieces each and add with sultanas to the bowl.

4 Add cereal. Peel apple and remove core. Grate apple and add to muesli mix.

5 Mix all ingredients together carefully and divide mixture into two serving bowls.

6 Serve with yogurt or milk poured on top.

recipe idea
Any dried or fresh fruit can be
used in this recipe.
Use a cereal of your own choice.

breakfasts

- **makes:** 600 ml (1 pt) ■ **preparation:** 10 minutes
- **cooking & cooling:** 30 minutes, plus 8–9 hours fermenting time

homemade yogurt

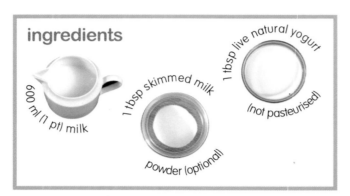

ingredients

600 ml (1 pt) milk

1 tbsp skimmed milk powder (optional)

1 tbsp live natural yogurt (not pasteurised)

1 Carefully rinse the vacuum flask and saucepan with boiling water.

2 Pour the milk into the saucepan and gently bring to the boil. Small bubbles will rise to the surface. To make a thicker yogurt, keep the milk on a very low heat for 15 minutes.

3 Remove pan from heat and put thermometer into milk. Cool to 45ºC (110ºF).

4 If using the milk powder, put into mixing bowl and add two or three spoons of the cooled milk. Add live yogurt. Mix until smooth. Pour in the remaining milk and stir.

5 Put the funnel into the vacuum flask and pour the milk mixture into the funnel. Put the lid on the flask and leave undisturbed for 8–9 hours.

6 Pour yogurt into small pots or cartons and refrigerate. It will keep for up to ten days.

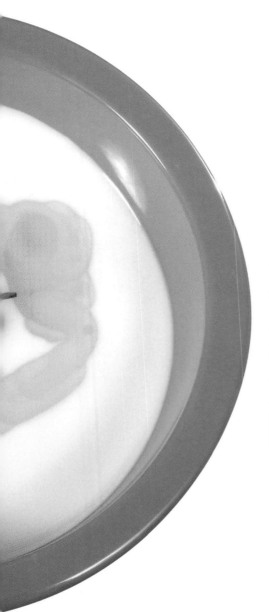

recipe ideas
Flavour the finished yogurt with honey or fresh, tinned or dried fruit.

recipe tip
To make another flask of yogurt, keep back a tablespoon of the yogurt you make. You can do this about three times and then use fresh natural yogurt.

breakfasts

- **makes:** 12
- **preparation:** 15 minutes
- **cooking:** 25 minutes
- **oven temperature:** 190°C (375°F/Gas mark 5)

fruit muffins

1 Preheat the oven. Brush the muffin tin with a little melted butter or oil.

ingredients

150 g (5 oz) self-raising flour

190 g (5½ oz) butter, melted

50 g (2 oz) caster sugar

2 eggs

2 tsp baking powder

150 g (5 oz) fresh, tinned or frozen berries, chopped if large

150 g (5 oz) wholemeal self-raising flour

350 ml (12 fl oz) milk or buttermilk

(blueberries, raspberries, loganberries, strawberries)

2 Sift the flour, sugar and baking powder into a bowl. Make a well in the centre.

3 In the measuring jug, mix together the eggs, milk and melted butter. Add to the bowl. Stir with a wooden spoon until almost smooth. The ingredients should be just mixed.

4 Add the berries.

5 Spoon mixture evenly into the muffin tin.

6 Bake for 20–25 minutes, or until golden brown. To test the muffins, insert a skewer in the centre of one – it should come out clean if they are ready. Loosen the muffins from the tin and cool on a wire rack.

recipe ideas
• For banana muffins, decrease the butter to 100 g (3¹/₂ oz) and add 240 g (8¹/₂ oz) mashed banana and 3 tsp grated orange rind instead of the berries.

• For chocolate-chip muffins, sift 2 tbsp cocoa powder in with the flour; add 225 g (8 oz) chopped chocolate or chocolate bits instead of the berries. Use white, milk or dark chocolate, or a mixture.

• For apple and date muffins, add 75 g (3 oz) chopped dates and 175 g (6 oz) grated eating apple instead of the berries.

recipe tip
The best muffins are made by not beating the mixture but stirring until just combined.

quick snacks & light meals

sweet potato & chilli soup

ingredients

2 medium leeks

25 g (1 oz) butter

700 g (1½ lb) sweet potatoes

1-2 tbsp chilli sauce

2 tbsp crème fraîche

Salt and Pepper

1.2 l (2 pt) vegetable stock

1 Peel leeks and cut off root. Remove outer leaves and, with a sharp knife, cut down the length of each leek and wash well under cold running water. Chop into small pieces.

2 In a saucepan, melt butter and add leek. Gently cook leek until soft, but not brown. Peel and slice sweet potatoes.

3 Add to saucepan. Cook for 2–3 minutes. Add stock. Bring to the boil and reduce until simmering. Cook for 25 minutes.

4 With a hand-held blender, whizz the soup until smooth. Beware of hot splashes! Season with salt and pepper.

5 Add 1 table-spoon chilli sauce and taste the soup to see if you would like a stronger flavour, adding more chilli sauce if liked.

6 Stir in creme fraiche.

prawn chowder

1 Peel and chop the onion and carrot. In a saucepan, melt the butter and add chopped vegetables, cover with a lid and cook slowly for 5–10 minutes, stirring occasionally.

ingredients

1 medium-sized onion

25 g (1 oz) butter

1.2 l (2 pt) fish stock

1 carrot

175 g (6 oz) shelled prawns

100 g (4 oz) sweet corn

800 g (1¾ lb) potatoes

150 ml (¼ pt) milk

50 g (2 oz) cheese (grated)

Salt and pepper

2 Add the stock to the saucepan and bring to the boil.

3 Meanwhile, peel potatoes and chop into even-sized chunks. Add the potato chunks to saucepan and simmer for 25 minutes, until the potato is cooked.

4 Add prawns, sweet corn, milk and seasoning. Simmer for a further 5 minutes. Ladle soup into bowls and sprinkle with grated cheese.

chicken noodle soup

ingredients

275 g (10 oz) chicken breasts

900 ml (1½ pt) chicken stock

1 tsp mild curry powder

50 g (2 oz) egg noodles

2 tbsp fresh chopped parsley

Salt and Pepper

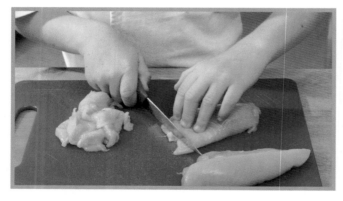

1 Slice chicken into thin strips. Put strips into a saucepan and add stock. Bring to the boil and simmer for 10 minutes.

2 Remove saucepan from the heat and, using a slotted spoon, transfer chicken to another saucepan, saving the stock. Add curry powder to chicken and cook for 2–3 minutes.

3 While the chicken and curry powder are still cooking, gradually add ladles of the stock until all is used.

4 Add noodles, parsley and seasoning. Simmer for 10 minutes and serve.

recipe idea
Soup is best served with crusty bread.

fruity chutney dip

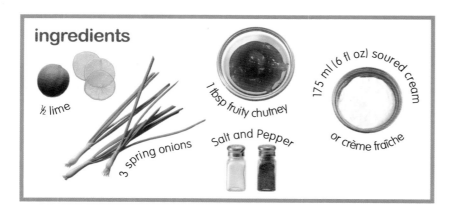

ingredients

½ lime

3 spring onions

1 tbsp fruity chutney

Salt and Pepper

175 ml (6 fl oz) soured cream or crème fraîche

1 Peel and chop spring onions into small pieces.

2 Squeeze lime juice into a bowl and add chopped spring onion and soured cream or crème fraîche.

3 Add fruity chutney and season with salt and pepper. Stir and put in a small serving bowl.

sun-dried tomato dip

ingredients

1 tomato

1-2 tbsp sun-dried tomato paste

200 g (7 oz) Greek yogurt

Salt and Pepper

1 Chop tomato into small pieces and put in a bowl with sun-dried tomato paste and Greek yogurt. Mix well and season with salt and pepper. Put in a small serving bowl.

recipe idea
There are many excellent dippers. Try the following:
- Carrot, celery, cucumber and peppers cut into sticks (called crudites).
- Pitta bread, toasted and cut into quarters.
- French stick cut into thin slices, lightly brushed with olive oil and crushed garlic, then popped in a medium oven until golden brown.
- Potato wedges.

quick snacks & light meals

- **serves:** 2 ■ **preparation:** 15 minutes ■ **cooking:** 15 minutes
- **oven temperature:** 200ºC (400ºF/Gas mark 6)

egg-stuffed tomatoes on toast

ingredients

Salt and Pepper

Sprig of parsley

2 large beef tomatoes

1 tbsp butter

150 ml (5 fl oz) double cream

50 g (2 oz) cheese (grated)

2 tbsp tomato sauce

2 large eggs

2 thick-cut slices bread, toasted

1 Slice a thin section off the top of each tomato and scrape out the insides with a teaspoon. Season each tomato inside with a little salt and pepper, turn upside down on a plate and leave for 5 minutes.

3 Break eggs and separate yolks and whites into separate bowls.

2 Finely chop parsley and add half to a small bowl, together with the cream and tomato sauce. Mix well.

4 Turn tomatoes over and carefully put an egg yolk inside each one.

5 Three-quarters fill each tomato with the cream mixture.

6 Divide the grated cheese between the two tomatoes and return tops to the tomatoes. Put on a baking tray and bake for 15 minutes.

7 While cooking the tomatoes, press a large cup or small bowl, upside down, into each slice of toast to make as large a circle as possible.

8 Put the remaining cream into a saucepan and heat until almost boiling. Put toast onto a serving plate, spread lightly with butter and place a tomato on top of each circle of toast. Drizzle cream around edges of toast and sprinkle with remaining chopped parsley. Serve.

59

■ **makes:** 8 pasties ■ **preparation:** 30 minutes ■ **cooking:** 45 minutes
■ **oven temperature:** 200°C (400°F/Gas mark 6)

pasties

ingredients - **pastry**

700 g (1½ lb) plain flour

175 ml (6 fl oz) cold water

350 g (12 oz) margarine

+ Extra water or milk

ingredients - **filling**

1 large onion

½ swede

2 carrots

450 g (1 lb) chuck steak or minced beef

1 large potato

1 egg

Salt and Pepper

1 Sift flour into a mixing bowl and add margarine. Rub in flour and margarine until mixture resembles fine breadcrumbs.

2 Add water a little at a time and mix with a fork until combined and stuck together, but not sticky.

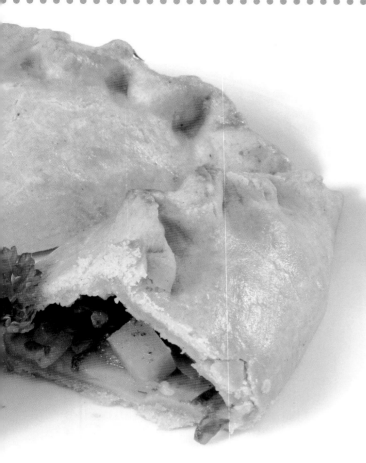

3 Peel and chop onion, swede and carrots into small pieces and put into separate bowls. Peel potato and slice thinly into small slithers. Put into bowl. If using chuck steak, cut into small chunks.

4 Using a sieve, sprinkle a small handful of flour onto a clean worktop, Divide the pastry into four pieces and roll each piece into a circular shape until 4 mm ($^{3}/_{16}$ in) thick.

5 Place a side plate, upside down, on each pastry circle and cut around the plate. Using a pastry brush, dampen the edges of each circle with water or milk.

6 On half of each circle, layer the potato, meat, onion and vegetables, leaving a 2.5 cm (1 in) gap around the edges. Sprinkle with salt and pepper.

7 Fold the uncovered half of the pastry over the filling to make a crescent shape and press the edges together.

8 Use your fingertips to pinch the edges to crimp them.

9 Using the tip of a knife, make a small slit in the centre of each pasty to let out steam.

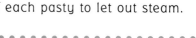

recipe ideas
Use white meat or grated cheese instead of beef.
Vegetables can be varied. Try leeks, peppers and sweet corn.

10 Break egg into a cup and mix with a fork. Brush each pasty with beaten egg and put onto baking tray. Bake.

food fact
The pasty was created in Cornwall, England, in the 1800s and was important in the diet of miners and farmers. They would have meat at one end of the pasty and fruit at the other to provide a complete meal. The pasty would be held by the crust when eaten so as not to get dirty hands all over the pastry and then the crust thrown away at the end of the meal.

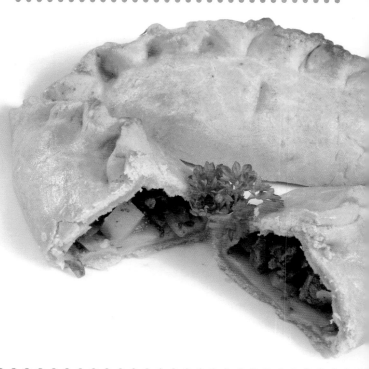

prawn & avocado tortilla wraps

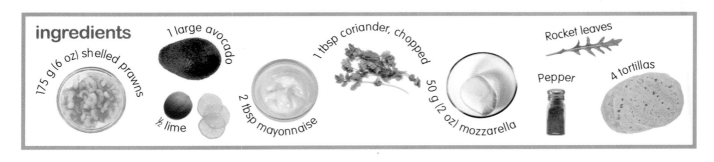

ingredients

175 g (6 oz) shelled prawns

1 large avocado

½ lime

2 tbsp mayonnaise

1 tbsp coriander, chopped

50 g (2 oz) mozzarella

Rocket leaves

Pepper

4 tortillas

1 Place prawns in a bowl and stir in mayonnaise.

2 Peel avocado and remove stone. Chop into small chunks.

3 Add to bowl.

4 Squeeze juice from lime and add to bowl. Stir to mix ingredients.

5 Chop coriander and add to bowl.

6 Chop mozzarella into small chunks and add to bowl. Mix until all ingredients are combined. Season with pepper.

7 Heat tortillas according to packet instructions. Place a layer of rocket leaves down centre of tortilla and top with prawn filling.

recipe idea
Another yummy tortilla filling is bean, vegetable and cheese. Make up your own!

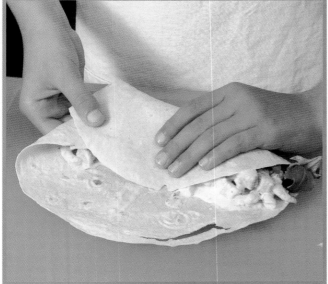

8 Take bottom edge of tortilla and fold a 2.5 cm (1 in) flap. Roll tortilla from one side to enclose filling.

beef chilli pitta bread

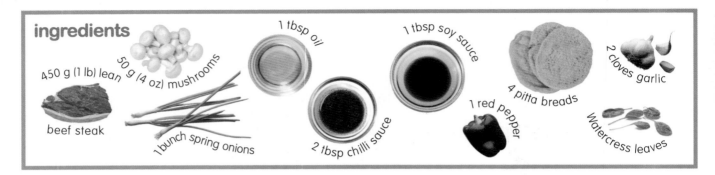

ingredients

450 g (1 lb) lean beef steak

50 g (4 oz) mushrooms

1 bunch spring onions

1 tbsp oil

2 tbsp chilli sauce

1 tbsp soy sauce

4 pitta breads

1 red pepper

2 cloves garlic

Watercress leaves

1 Slice steak into thin strips. Peel and crush garlic cloves.

2 Heat oil in frying pan, add meat and garlic and cook for 3–4 minutes until brown. Remove meat, using a slotted spoon, and place in a bowl.

3 Peel and chop spring onions and mushrooms. Add these to the frying pan and cook for 2–3 minutes, adding a little more oil to the frying pan if the ingredients start to stick.

4 Deseed and chop the red pepper into chunks. Add to frying pan with soy sauce and chilli sauce. Add more or less chilli sauce according to your taste.

recipe idea
Vary meat by using lamb cutlets and top with a sauce made from 8 tbsp Greek yogurt and 2 tbsp mint sauce.

5 Return beef to frying pan and heat for 2–3 minutes. Meanwhile, heat pitta bread according to packet instructions. Leave to cool for 1 minute and cut each pitta bread in half.

6 Put watercress into colander and rinse under cold running water, then shake gently. Fill each pitta pocket with cooked chilli beef and top with watercress.

- **serves:** 2 - **preparation:** 15 minutes - **cooking:** 30–40 minutes
- **marinating:** 1 hour - **oven:** 220°C (425°F/Gas mark 7)

lemon chicken baguette

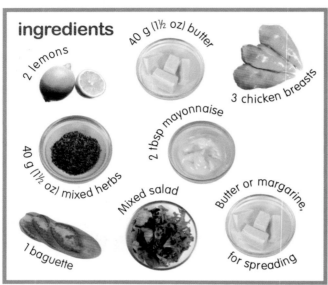

ingredients

2 lemons

40 g (1½ oz) butter

3 chicken breasts

2 tbsp mayonnaise

40 g (1½ oz) mixed herbs

Mixed salad

Butter or margarine, for spreading

1 baguette

1 Zest lemon rind into a bowl. Cut lemons in half and use a lemon-squeezer to extract the juices into the bowl with the zest, making sure there are no pips.

2 Soak the chicken breasts in lemon zest and juices for 1 hour in the fridge. Put the butter in a roasting tray with deep sides and place in the oven for 5 minutes until the butter has melted.

3 Add chicken, zest and lemon juice to the melted butter, and add herbs. Cover with tin foil and place in oven for 30-40 minutes.

4 Leave to cool and then slice the chicken into thin strips.

5 Put into a bowl with the mayonnaise and mix well.

6 Cut the baguette in half and spread with butter or margarine. Fill with chicken mixture and top with mixed salad.

recipe idea
Omit the mayonnaise and put sliced meat on a plate with a fruity salad – try orange segments, sultanas, chopped apricots, mixed lettuce leaves, tomatoes and cucumber.

beef double-decker sandwich

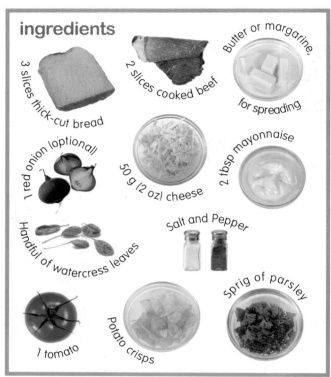

ingredients

3 slices thick-cut bread

2 slices cooked beef

Butter or margarine, for spreading

1 red onion (optional)

50 g (2 oz) cheese

2 tbsp mayonnaise

Handful of watercress leaves

Salt and Pepper

Sprig of parsley

1 tomato

Potato crisps

1 Spread each slice of bread with butter or margarine, making sure it is spread to the edges of each slice.

2 Put the slices of beef onto one slice of bread. If adding red onion, peel and slice two rounds thinly, then sprinkle onto beef.

3 Place the second slice of bread, butter side down, onto beef and spoon some mayonnaise on top of the sandwich. Spread mayonnaise to the edges.

4 Slice cheese and place on mayonnaise. Slice tomatoes and place on top of cheese.

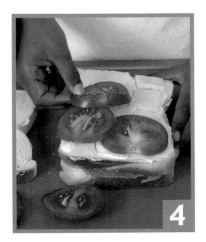

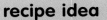

5 Sprinkle with salt and pepper, add watercress leaves to the sandwich and top with the remaining piece of bread.

6 Cut the sandwich into four quarters and put them onto a plate. Add a handful of crisps to the sides of the plate and decorate the sandwich with a sprig of parsley.

recipe idea
Choose any two fillings that will mix together – any meat, fish, egg or salad can be used. Also try different salad dressings, mustard or relish.

■ **serves:** 4 ■ **preparation:** 15 minutes ■ **cooking:** 1½–2 hours
■ **oven temperature:** 200°C (400°F/Gas mark 7)

stuffed golden jacket potatoes

1 Wash the potatoes and dry on some kitchen towels. Put the potatoes on a baking tray and bake for 1–1½ hours until they are soft when a skewer is inserted.

ingredients

4 potatoes
1 small onion
1 red pepper
100 g (4 oz) coloured mature cheese
Black Pepper
1 tbsp oil
4 tbsp milk
Worcestershire sauce
2 tbsp sweet corn

2 Cut the potatoes in half and, using a spoon, scoop out the insides of the potatoes, just leaving a shell (save these). Put the scooped-out potato into a bowl and mash.

3 Peel the onion and finely chop. Deseed and chop the pepper.

4 Put oil into a frying pan and heat. Add chopped onion and pepper and cook gently, stirring with a spatula, for 5 minutes. Add sweet corn and milk and heat gently.

5 Add this mixture to the mashed potato. Grate cheese and add half of it to the potato mixture, along with Worcestershire sauce and a sprinkle of black pepper.

recipe idea
Add chopped cooked meat or fish at step 4, if preferred.

6 Turn on the grill. Pile the mixture back into the potato shells and sprinkle over remaining cheese. Place potatoes under the grill until golden brown.

■ **serves:** 4 ■ **preparation:** 15 minutes ■ **cooking:** 1–1½ hours
■ **oven temperature:** 200°C (400°F/Gas mark 7)

jacket potato with coronation chicken

ingredients

450 g (1 lb) chicken breast • 4 potatoes • 175 g (6 oz) crème fraîche • 1 tsp curry paste • Salt and Pepper • 1 tbsp mango chutney • 2 tsp sultanas

1 Wash the potatoes and dry on some kitchen towel. Put potatoes in the oven on a baking tray for 1–1½ hours until soft and a skewer can be inserted easily.

2 Meanwhile, put chicken breast in a casserole dish with 2 tbsp water and a light sprinkle of salt and pepper. Cover with a lid and bake in the oven for 30 minutes, until cooked.

3 Remove chicken breasts from the casserole dish and leave to cool on a chopping board. Slice chicken into 1-cm (½-in) thick slices.

4 To a bowl, add crème fraîche, curry paste, mango chutney and sultanas. Stir until well combined.

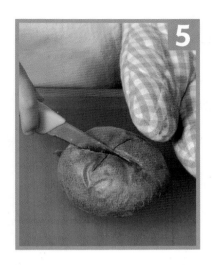

5 When the potato is cooked, slice an 'X' across the top of the potato skin and gently push down on the four edges of each potato to open it slightly.

6 Mix the sliced chicken into curry sauce and spoon into each potato.

recipe idea
Add chopped apple to curry sauce to give it extra crunch.

■ **serves:** 4 ■ **preparation:** 30 minutes, plus 30 minutes chilling time
■ **cooking:** 30 minutes

chicken goujons

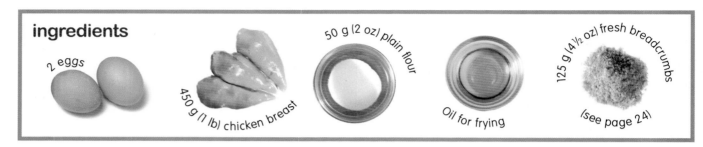

ingredients

2 eggs

450 g (1 lb) chicken breast

50 g (2 oz) plain flour

Oil for frying

125 g (4½ oz) fresh breadcrumbs (see page 24)

1 Cut the chicken breast into long thin strips. Put the flour into a plastic food bag and add the chicken strips.

2 Hold the bag firmly and shake until all the chicken is evenly coated with flour.

3 Using tongs, remove the chicken from the bag, shaking off the excess flour.

4 Beat the eggs in a bowl and put the bread-crumbs into a plastic food bag.

recipe idea
Serve with stir-fried vegetables or your favourite sauce.

5 Using tongs, dip a few strips of the chicken into the egg and then add to the bag of breadcrumbs. Shake to cover chicken with crumbs. Put the chicken onto a plate and repeat the process with the remaining chicken. Put the chicken in the fridge to chill for 30 minutes.

6 Heat 1 cm ($\frac{1}{2}$ in) oil in a frying pan until hot. Add chicken and fry for 5 minutes or until golden brown and cooked through, turning the chicken often.

pizza, pasta & rice

pizza, pasta & rice

■ **serves:** 6 ■ **preparation:** 20–25 minutes ■ **cooking:** 20–25 minutes
■ **oven temperature:** 200°C (400°F/Gas mark 6)

chicken & sweet-corn pizza

ingredients -
scone base

400 g (14 oz) self-raising flour

100 g (4 oz) margarine

2 eggs

2 tbsp flour

Topping

200 g (7 oz) passata

75 g (3 oz) button mushrooms

175 g (6 oz) chicken breast

4 tbsp sweet corn

½ red pepper

175 g (6 oz) mozzarella

2 tsp oregano

1 Sieve flour into mixing bowl and add margarine. Rub margarine into flour between your fingers and thumb until the mixture looks like small breadcrumbs. Add eggs and combine with a fork until the dough is stuck together.

2 Sprinkle 2 tablespoons flour onto worktop and gently roll dough out in a circle shape until 3 cm (1½ in) thick. Put pizza base on a greased baking tray.

3 Spread pizza base with passata. Chop chicken breast into 1 cm (½ in) cubes, and put into clean mixing bowl.

4 Using a clean chopping board and knife, remove any seeds from red pepper and slice into strips. Add to bowl. Peel and slice button mushrooms. Add to bowl.

5 Cut mozzarella into small cubes and add to bowl, along with sweet corn. Mix ingredients together. Top pizza base with mix, then sprinkle with oregano.

6 Bake pizza for 20–25 minutes until brown and chicken pieces are white all the way through when cut in half.

recipe idea
Try adding 3 rashers of bacon to mixture at step 3.

Use a few fresh basil leaves instead of oregano.

- **serves:** 6   - **preparation:** 15 minutes + 1 hour 30–40 minutes proving time
- **cooking:** 10–15 minutes   - **oven temperature:** 240°C (475°F/Gas mark 9)

spinach & tomato pizza

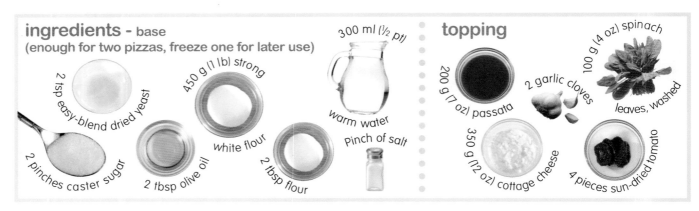

ingredients - base
(enough for two pizzas, freeze one for later use)

2 tsp easy-blend dried yeast

2 pinches caster sugar

450 g (1 lb) strong white flour

2 tbsp olive oil

2 tbsp flour

300 ml (½ pt) warm water

Pinch of salt

topping

200 g (7 oz) passata

2 garlic cloves

100 g (4 oz) spinach leaves, washed

350 g (12 oz) cottage cheese

4 pieces sun-dried tomato

1 Sprinkle yeast and sugar over warm water in a small bowl and leave to stand for 20 minutes until frothy.

2 Sieve the flour into a large bowl and add a pinch of salt. Pour in yeast mixture and olive oil.

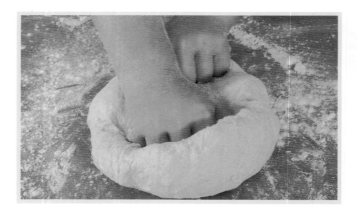

3 Mix to soft dough and knead for 5 minutes until smooth and elastic. Cover with oiled plastic wrap and leave in a warm place for 1 hour to rise until double in size.

4 Sprinkle 2 tbsp flour onto worktop and punch the dough flat, cut in half and roll out each half until 30 cm (12 in) across. Let dough rise for 15 minutes.

5 Grease baking tray with oil and put base onto the tray and spread with passata. Cut spinach leaves into fine strips and sprinkle over base.

6 Peel garlic cloves and crush. Sprinkle over base and top with cottage cheese. Cut sun-dried tomatoes into strips and sprinkle over pizza. Bake in oven for 10–15 minutes.

- **serves:** 2 ■ **preparation:** 20 minutes ■ **cooking:** 15–20 minutes
- **oven temperature:** 180°C (350°F/Gas mark 4)

easy mini-muffin pizza

ingredients

2 bread muffins

1 cloves garlic

1 tbsp Parmesan cheese

3 tbsp tomato purée

2 slices meat

1 tomato

2 mushrooms

½ red pepper

50 g (2 ozl cheese (grated)

1 Cover base of baking tray with foil. Cut muffins in half and put on baking tray.

2 Crush garlic and put in mixing bowl with Parmesan cheese and tomato purée. Stir until smooth.

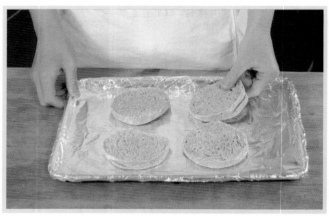

3 Spread mixture evenly over bread.

4 Slice pepper into strips.

5 Chop tomato into small pieces and thinly slice mushrooms. Arrange vegetables on pizza bases.

6 Slice meat into strips and sprinkle on pizza. Top with grated cheese. Bake in oven until the cheese has melted and the bases are crisp.

recipe idea
Try different types of bread: pitta bread, flat bread, naan bread and baguette.

beef strips with vegetable couscous

ingredients

450 g (1 lb) sirloin steak

1 Orange

1 tbsp olive oil

1 tbsp ground cumin

1 yellow pepper

425 g (15 oz) tin chickpeas

175 g (6 oz) mange tout

1 red pepper

225 g (8 oz) couscous

2 red onions

300 ml (½ pt) coconut milk

600 ml (1 pt) boiling chicken stock

2 tbsp fresh coriander

1 Slice steak into thin strips, heat olive oil in frying pan and cook for 3–4 minutes until browned.

2 Remove beef using slotted spoon and put to one side. Keep juices from meat in the frying pan.

3 Put the couscous in a bowl and pour over 450 ml
(16 fl oz) chicken stock to cover ingredients. Leave
for 5–10 minutes until liquid is absorbed.
Use a fork to break up any lumps
of couscous.

4 Peel onions and cut into slices. Remove cores and
seeds from peppers and thinly slice. Fry onions and
peppers in the frying pan for 10 minutes.

5 Add the cumin and cook for 2 minutes. Meanwhile,
grate the rind of the orange.

6 Then squeeze the juice.

7 Add rind and juice to frying pan, along with the remaining stock, mange tout, chickpeas and coconut milk. Bring to the boil and simmer for 5 minutes.

8 Return cooked beef strips to frying pan with the couscous. Chop coriander leaves and add to pan. Heat thoroughly and serve.

recipe idea
Try chicken or sausages instead of sirloin steak.

food fact
Couscous is produced by moistening grains of semolina and making them into tiny pellets coated with fine wheat flour. It is a staple food in North African countries.

tuna lasagne

ingredients

3 tbsp tomato purée

50 g (4 oz) mushrooms

2 x 450 g (15 oz) tins chopped tomatoes

1 medium-sized onion

1 x 400 g (14 oz) tin tuna

2 cloves garlic

2 tsp mixed herbs

6–8 sheets lasagne

2 tsp Worcestershire sauce

sauce

600 ml (1 pt) semi-skimmed or full-fat milk

25 g (1 oz) butter

275 g (10 oz) cheese

25 g (1 oz) plain flour

Salt and pepper

1 Peel and chop onion. Peel and crush clove of garlic. Heat oil in frying pan and gently cook for 3–4 minutes until soft, but not brown.

2 Peel and slice mushrooms, add to frying pan and cook for 2 minutes.

3 Drain any liquid from tin of tuna and add to frying pan with chopped tomatoes, tomato purée, Worcestershire sauce and mixed herbs.

4 Bring to boil and simmer for 10 minutes. Meanwhile, place the milk, butter and flour in a saucepan. Gently bring to the boil, whisking continually. Simmer for 1 minute.

5 Grate cheese and add three-quarters of it to sauce with a pinch of salt and pepper.

6 Pour half of the tuna mixture into an ovenproof baking dish, cover with a single layer of lasagne sheets, then half of the cheese-sauce mixture.

7 Repeat with remaining tuna mix, lasagne sheets and cheese sauce.

8 Sprinkle reserved grated cheese on top and bake until golden.

recipe idea
Serve with salad and
garlic bread.

turkey creole

ingredients

225 g (8 oz) long-grain brown rice

600 ml (1 pt) boiling vegetable stock

400 g (14 oz) tin chopped tomatoes

1 tsp mixed herbs

1 tbsp plain flour

2 tbsp Worcestershire sauce

2 cloves garlic

1 red onion

450 g (1 lb) turkey breast

1 tbsp oil

100 g (4 oz) frozen peas

1 red pepper

100 g (4 oz) mushrooms

1 Put rice in a saucepan with water and stock cube. Bring to the boil, reduce heat and simmer for 20 minutes or until the rice is tender and the water has been absorbed. Stir occasionally.

2 Meanwhile, slice turkey breast into thin strips.

3 Heat oil in frying pan and cook turkey for 5 minutes until cooked. Remove meat from frying pan with slotted spoon and put in a bowl. Keep juices in frying pan.

4 Using a clean chopping board and knife, peel and finely chop the onion. Peel clove of garlic and crush it. Add both to frying pan. Deseed and dice the pepper.

5 Start to fry onion, garlic and pepper. Slice mushrooms and add to pan.

6 Fry until ingredients are soft, but not browned. Stir in the flour and cook for 2 minutes. Add tomatoes, herbs, Worcestershire sauce and peas. Bring to the boil, cover pan with a lid and simmer for 10 minutes.

7 Add turkey and rice and cook for 5 minutes. Divide between four plates and serve immediately.

recipe idea
Use a fish mixture, either 400 g (14 oz) tin tuna or 450 g (1 lb) mixed seafood.

thai noodles

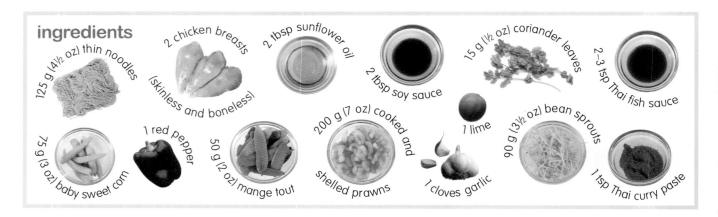

ingredients

125 g (4½ oz) thin noodles

2 chicken breasts (skinless and boneless)

2 tbsp sunflower oil

2 tbsp soy sauce

15 g (½ oz) coriander leaves

2–3 tsp Thai fish sauce

75 g (3 oz) baby sweet corn

1 red pepper

50 g (2 oz) mange tout

200 g (7 oz) cooked and shelled prawns

1 lime

1 cloves garlic

90 g (3½ oz) bean sprouts

1 tsp Thai curry paste

1 Put noodles into a bowl and cover with boiling water. Leave to stand for 4 minutes, then drain noodles using the colander.

2 Thinly slice chicken breasts. Heat oil in wok, add sliced chicken and stir-fry over a high heat for 4 minutes. Remove seeds and core from the pepper and thinly slice.

3 Add pepper, baby sweet corn and mange tout and cook for 2 minutes. Peel garlic clove and crush. Add to wok.

4 Stir in soy sauce, bean sprouts and prawns. Stir-fry for 1 minute.

5 Chop coriander leaves and add to wok, along with cooked noodles. Sir-fry for 1–2 minutes.

6 Add fish sauce and curry paste and stir-fry for 1 minute. Cut lime into 4 wedges. Spoon noodle mixture into dishes and decorate each with coriander leaves and a wedge of lime.

recipe idea
Use different vegetables, such as spring onions, thinly sliced carrots or sliced courgette.

pepperoni pasta

ingredients

175 g (6 oz) pepperoni sausage

275 g (10 oz) dried pasta

100 g (4 oz) cherry tomatoes

100 g (4 oz) tin baby sweet corn

15 g (½ oz) fresh chives

3 tbsp red pesto

1 red onion

150 ml (½ pt) crème fraîche

1 Half fill a saucepan with water and bring to the boil. Add pasta and follow packet instructions for the cooking time.

2 Meanwhile, slice the pepperoni and red onion. Heat frying pan (without oil) and cook onion and sausage together until onion is soft.

3 In a bowl, mix pesto and crème fraîche together.

4 Add this to the frying pan and stir well.

5 Chop cherry tomatoes in half and drain any liquid from the tin of sweet corn. Add these ingredients to frying pan and stir. Snip chives with a pair of scissors into 6mm (¼ in) pieces.

6 Drain pasta and pour into frying pan with sauce. Stir gently until all ingredients are combined. Serve. Sprinkle with chives.

recipe idea
Use other meat, such as chicken or turkey breast.
Try adding mushrooms and peppers at step 2.

vegetables
& salads

■ **serves:** 4 ■ **preparation:** 20 minutes ■ **cooking:** 45 minutes
■ **oven temperature:** 220°C (425°F/Gas mark 7)

potato wedges

ingredients

8 medium-sized baking potatoes

3 tbsp olive oil

100 g (4 oz) mature cheese

Salt and Pepper

1 Scrub each potato clean with water and a nailbrush and pat dry with kitchen roll.

2 Cut each potato in half, then quarters, and then cut each quarter in half again (to give eight wedges per potato).

3 Put an empty roasting tin into the oven to heat for 5 minutes. In a bowl, mix oil and seasoning together and add potato wedges.

4 Toss potatoes in oil until well coated.

5 Grate cheese. Remove hot roasting tin carefully from oven and pour potato wedges into tin in a single layer.

6 Sprinkle with cheese and bake until crispy and brown. Shake tin occasionally during cooking time to prevent wedges sticking.

recipe idea
Wedges are great served with burgers or as an alternative to chips. Also use to dip in sour cream or houmous.

ratatouille

ingredients

1 large onion

1 red pepper

1 large aubergine

400 g (14 oz) tin chopped tomatoes

225 g (8 oz) courgettes

150 ml (¼ pt) water

2 tbsp oil

1 green pepper

2 cloves garlic

225 g (8 oz) tomatoes

2 tbsp tomato purée

2 tsp mixed herbs

Salt and Pepper

1 Peel and slice onion. Peel and crush garlic.

2 Cut top and tail off aubergine and dice. Remove stalks from peppers and deseed, then slice into thin strips.

3 Slice courgettes and tomatoes. Heat oil in the frying pan or wok and start gently to cook onion and garlic until soft, but not brown.

4 Add sliced peppers and aubergine and cook for 2 minutes.

Add courgettes, sliced tomatoes and chopped tomatoes and cook for 2 minutes. Stir in water, tomato purée and mixed herbs and season with salt and pepper. Put a lid on the pan and simmer gently for 20 minutes, stirring occasionally.

vegetables & salads

- **serves:** 4 - **preparation:** 25 minutes plus 30 minutes salting time
- **cooking:** 40 minutes - **oven temperature:** 200°C (400°F/Gas mark 6)

roasted vegetables

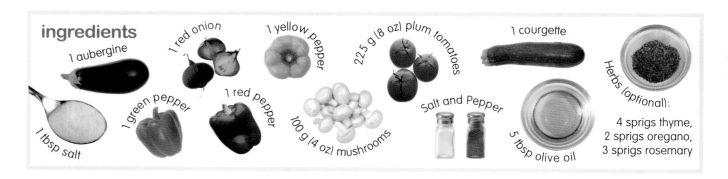

ingredients

1 aubergine

1 tbsp salt

1 green pepper

1 red onion

1 red pepper

1 yellow pepper

100 g (4 oz) mushrooms

225 g (8 oz) plum tomatoes

Salt and Pepper

1 courgette

5 tbsp olive oil

Herbs (optional):
4 sprigs thyme,
2 sprigs oregano,
3 sprigs rosemary

1 Cut top and tail off aubergine and cut into large chunks. Put on a plate and sprinkle with salt. Leave for 30 minutes.

2 Meanwhile, prepare the vegetables. Deseed the peppers and cut into thick strips. Trim top and bottom off the courgette and cut into large chunks.

3 Peel the onion and cut into thick slices. Cut the tomatoes into quarters.

4 Squeeze the aubergine chunks to remove as much liquid as you can. Rinse under a running tap and put into a roasting tray.

5 Arrange remaining vegetables in roasting tray and drizzle oil over them.

6 If using herbs, sprinkle in among the vegetables and season all with salt and pepper. Put the roasting tray in oven for 40 minutes, turning vegetables over halfway through.

food fact
Salting aubergine stops it from tasting bitter. The salt draws out bitter juices and helps to stop the aubergine absorbing too much oil during cooking.

cheesy salad

1 Prepare all the vegetables: finely chop cabbages; peel and slice carrots; peel and cut mushrooms into quarters; cut potatoes in half; cut off ends of courgette and grate (use coarse grater); cut cucumber into 50-mm (¼-in) cubes; roughly chop tomatoes.

ingredients

¼ small white cabbage
¼ small red cabbage
8 baby carrots
100 g (4 oz) cooked new potatoes
50 g (4 oz) mushrooms
50 g (2 oz) sweet corn
50 g (2 oz) bean sprouts
1 tbsp lemon juice
2 tbsp olive oil
1 small courgette
3 tomatoes
50–100 g (2–4 oz) cheese
Bread Rolls
Salt and Pepper
10-cm (4-in) piece cucumber

2 Put prepared vegetables into a bowl and add bean sprouts. Mix together until well combined.

3 Stir in sweet corn and then drizzle over oil and lemon juice.

4 Season ingredients with salt and pepper and leave to stand for 30 minutes.

5 Grate cheese and sprinkle over salad when ready to serve. Slice crusty bread into four and serve.

recipe idea
Vary the vegetables depending on season and your own favourites.

chicken cocktail

ingredients

100 g (4 oz) cooked chicken
50 g (2 oz) button mushrooms
100 g (4 oz) small tomatoes
50 g (2 oz) ham
50 g (2 oz) green pepper
Salt and Pepper
50 g (2 oz) cheese
1 tbsp chopped parsley
100 g (4 oz) cucumber
1 tsp wine vinegar
lettuce
¼ tsp dried basil

ingredients - dressing

1 tbsp crème fraîche
2 tbsp mayonnaise
1 tbsp lemon juice
1 tsp honey
Water (if needed)

1 Wash the lettuce leaves in a colander using clean water and then shake to dry leaves. Use lettuce to line four wine glasses. Slice tomatoes and arrange three-quarters of the slices over the lettuce. Season lightly with salt and pepper.

2 Chop chicken into small cubes and divide it between the four glasses. Thinly slice cucumber and mushrooms. Deseed and thinly slice the pepper.

3 Put cucumber, mushrooms and pepper into a bowl. Add half of the parsley to the bowl of vegetables, along with basil and vinegar. Add salt and pepper, toss ingredients gently and spoon ingredients into glasses.

4 Cut ham into strips, grate cheese and divide between glasses.

5 To make dressing, beat all ingredients except the water together. If dressing is too thick to pour, add a little water.

6 Spoon dressing into the glasses and garnish with the remaining tomatoes and parsley.

recipe idea
Try beef or turkey or use a vegetarian alternative, such as Quorn fillet.

coleslaw

ingredients

340 g (¾ lb) white cabbage

3–4 spring onions

2 tbsp mayonnaise

Salt and Pepper

1 tbsp live natural yogurt

1½ tbsp salad cream

2 carrots

Few fresh chives for garnish

1 Peel outer leaves from cabbage and shred cabbage as finely as possible. Put in mixing bowl. Peel and grate carrots and add them to the bowl.

2 Peel and chop spring onions. Add to bowl, along with mayonnaise, yogurt and salad cream. Season with salt and pepper. Mix well. Transfer coleslaw to a serving bowl. Chop chives into 1 cm (½ in) pieces and sprinkle on top.

recipe tip
A fruity salad can be made by adding pineapple chunks, chopped apricots and sultanas with ½ tbsp honey.

waldorf salad

ingredients

1 tbsp lemon juice

2 eating apples, washed and dried

1 head celery

3 tbsp mayonnaise

3 tbsp sultanas

1 tbsp natural yogurt

1 Remove outer celery stalks and trim off base. Chop each stalk into 1 cm (¹/₂ in) pieces and add to mixing bowl.

2 Leaving apple skin on, cut each apple into quarters and remove core. Slice each quarter into 6 mm (¹/₄ in) slices. Add to bowl with lemon juice and mix.

3 Sprinkle sultanas into bowl and stir in mayonnaise and yogurt. Transfer salad to clean serving bowl.

recipe tip

If there are no known nut allergies, add 2 tbsp roughly chopped walnuts.

dressings - tomato & olive

ingredients

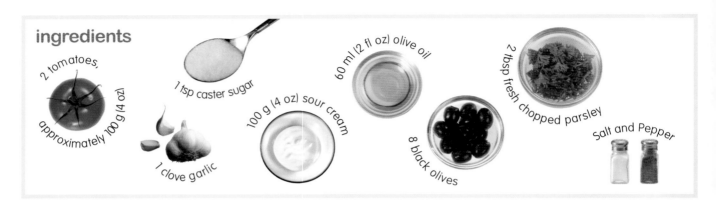

2 tomatoes, approximately 100 g (4 oz)

1 tsp caster sugar

1 clove garlic

100 g (4 oz) sour cream

60 ml (2 fl oz) olive oil

8 black olives

2 tbsp fresh chopped parsley

Salt and Pepper

1 Half fill a saucepan with water and bring to the boil. Use a slotted spoon to lower tomatoes into water for 30 seconds, then remove and put on a chopping board. When tomatoes are cool enough to touch, pierce skins with a small 'X' on the base and peel off skin. Cut tomatoes in half and use a teaspoon to scoop out seeds and discard them.

2 Rest sieve over a mixing bowl and push the tomatoes through the sieve using a wooden spoon. Stir in sugar, sour cream and oil.

3 Peel and crush clove of garlic, chop olives and parsley and add to bowl. Stir well. Season with salt and pepper.

dressings - egg & cress

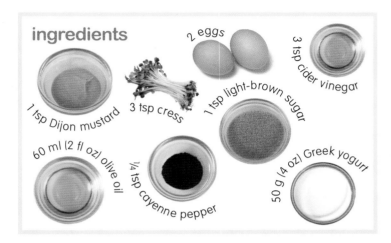

ingredients

2 eggs

3 tsp cider vinegar

1 tsp light-brown sugar

1 tsp Dijon mustard

3 tsp cress

60 ml (2 fl oz) olive oil

¼ tsp cayenne pepper

50 g (4 oz) Greek yogurt

recipe tip
Serve these dressings with meat, fish, rice, pasta or salads.

1 Fill a saucepan two-thirds full of water, put in eggs and bring to the boil. Reduce heat to simmer eggs for 10–12 minutes. Remove eggs with a slotted spoon and place under cold running water. Tap the shells and leave to cool before cracking the shell all over and peeling off.

2 Press eggs through a sieve over a mixing bowl using a tablespoon.

3 Add sugar, cayenne pepper, mustard and oil. Beat well until slightly thick and cloudy. Stir in yogurt and cress. Keep in fridge until needed.

greek-style salad

ingredients

3 tomatoes

½ cucumber

1 green pepper

225 g (8 oz) feta cheese

½ red onion

8 black olives

3–4 tbsp olive oil

Salt and Pepper

½ lettuce, e.g., cos lettuce

½ lemon

1 Remove stalks from tomatoes and cut each into eight wedges. Put into bowl.

2 Cut and deseed pepper and cut into small chunks. Add to bowl.

3 Cut cucumber into slices, and each slice into quarters. Add to bowl.

4 Cut feta cheese into 1 cm (½ in) lengths, then into cubes. Put into bowl.

5 Peel onion and cut thin slices to create rings. Add to bowl with olives. Rinse lettuce leaves under running water in a colander and then shake off excess water. Put in bowl.

6 Sprinkle salad with salt and pepper and drizzle lemon juice and oil over salad. Stir gently to mix and then serve.

main meals

main meals

■ **serves:** 4 ■ **preparation:** 15 minutes ■ **cooking:** 40 minutes
■ **oven temperature:** 180°C (350°F/Gas mark 4)

meatballs with tomato sauce

ingredients - meatballs

450 g (1 lb) minced beef

1 tbsp mixed herbs

25 g (1 oz) breadcrumbs (see page 24)

1 egg

Salt and Pepper

25 g (1 oz) Parmesan cheese

ingredients - sauce

1 tbsp oil

1 clove garlic

1 yellow pepper

1 onion

1 tbsp chopped parsley

400 g (14 oz) tin chopped tomatoes

350 g (12 oz) long spaghetti

1 Place all meatball ingredients in a bowl and mix with a spoon until well combined.

2 Use your hands to roll mixture into 10 balls. Put balls into a casserole dish and cook, uncovered, for 10 minutes.

3 Peel and chop onion. Peel clove of garlic and crush.

4 In a saucepan, heat the oil and cook onion and garlic gently until soft. Meanwhile, slice pepper and add to saucepan. Cook for a further 2–3 minutes.

5 Add chopped tomatoes, parsley and seasoning and bring to the boil.

6 Using a ladle, pour sauce over meatballs. Cook (with a lid on) for 20 minutes.

7 While the meatballs are cooking, boil a saucepan of water and cook spaghetti according to packet instructions.

recipe idea
Alternatively, serve with brown rice or mashed potato. Minced beef can be replaced with any minced meat or vegetarian mince.

main meals

■ **serves:** 4   ■ **preparation:** 10–15 minutes   ■ **marinating:** 30 minutes or overnight in fridge
■ **cooking:** 30 minutes   ■ **oven temperature:** 200°C (400°F/Gas mark 6)

marinated chicken

ingredients

½ Orange

½ lemon

1 tbsp balsamic vinegar

1 tsp oregano (dried or fresh)

4 tbsp tomato purée

Salt and Pepper

1 tbsp clear honey

4 chicken breasts

700 g (1½ lb) new potatoes

Mixed salad

1 Grate the rind of the orange and lemon and put into an ovenproof dish. Squeeze the juices and add to dish. Stir in the honey, balsamic vinegar, tomato purée, oregano and seasoning.

2 On each chicken breast, score lines 2.5 cm (1 in) apart with the tip of a sharp knife.

3 Add chicken pieces to marinade and spoon sauce all over chicken breasts until well covered. Cover dish with plastic wrap and marinate for at least 30 minutes.

4 Meanwhile, preheat the oven. Scrub new potatoes with a nailbrush and water to clean and remove loose skin.

5 Cook chicken for 30 minutes. Boil half a saucepan of water, carefully add new potatoes and cook for 15–20 minutes. The chicken and potatoes should be ready at the same time, so test both with a sharp knife to make sure potatoes are soft and chicken juices run clear.

6 Drain new potatoes in a colander and divide between serving plates. Add chicken and serve with a mixed salad.

recipe idea
These chicken breasts can be served cold in a salad or on a picnic.

fish & vegetable pie

ingredients

175 g (6 oz) spinach, rinsed under clean water

3 eggs

450 g (1 lb) white fish

100 g (4 oz) sweet corn

3 carrots

ingredients - sauce

600 ml (1 pt) milk

50 g (2 oz) butter

50 g (2 oz) plain flour

Salt and pepper

Topping

700 g (1½ lb) potatoes

100 g (4 oz) cheese (grated)

1   Put the eggs into a saucepan and cover with cold water. Bring to the boil and reduce heat to simmer the eggs for 5 minutes. Remove eggs with a slotted spoon and leave to cool in a bowl of cold water.

2   Fill a saucepan two-thirds full of water and bring to the boil. Reduce heat to simmer the water. Place spinach in a colander and rest over the saucepan for 5 minutes to wilt the spinach.

3   Remove from heat and put to one side, resting the colander on a plate.

4 Keeping the saucepan of water on heat, peel and chop carrots and add to water. Boil for 15 minutes, until cooked.

5 Meanwhile, put the fish into a saucepan and cover with milk from the sauce ingredients. Bring to the boil and reduce heat to simmer the fish for 15 minutes, until the fish flesh is white and firm.

6 Place fish in ovenproof dish.

7 Remove any skin or bones. Add remaining sauce ingredients to milk. Return saucepan to the heat and whisk sauce until it has boiled and thickened.

8 Add spinach to ovenproof dish and use colander to drain carrots. Boil a saucepan of water, peel potatoes and slice into 1 cm (½ in) slices. Cook for 10 minutes until tender.

9 Peel shells from eggs and cut eggs into quarters. Put into ovenproof dish with carrots and sweet corn. Pour over white sauce.

10 Place a row of cooked potato slices over the pie, and layer rows until the whole pie is covered. Sprinkle grated cheese on top and pop dish into the oven for 40 minutes until golden brown.

recipe tip: Serve with peas or any other cooked vegetables.

124

- **serves:** 4 ■ **preparation:** 30 minutes ■ **cooking:** 35–40 minutes
- **oven temperature:** 200°C (400°F/Gas mark 6)

moussaka

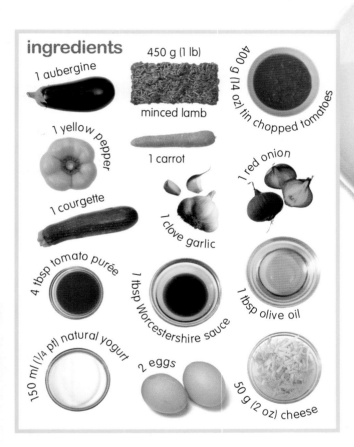

ingredients

1 aubergine

450 g (1 lb) minced lamb

400 g (14 oz) tin chopped tomatoes

1 yellow pepper

1 carrot

1 red onion

1 courgette

1 clove garlic

4 tbsp tomato purée

1 tbsp Worcestershire sauce

1 tbsp olive oil

150 ml (¼ pt) natural yogurt

2 eggs

50 g (2 oz) cheese

1 Prepare the aubergine. Slice into 1 cm (½ in) slices and salt for 30–40 minutes (see page 19).

2 Peel and crush the garlic. Peel and chop the onion. Put these ingredients into a saucepan with minced lamb and stir until softened and going brown.

3 Peel and grate the carrot and grate the courgette (skin on). Deseed the pepper and chop. Add these vegetables to the saucepan with chopped tomatoes and cook for 10 minutes. Stir in tomato purée and Worcestershire sauce. Place the mince mixture into an ovenproof dish.

4 Heat oil in a frying pan and quickly fry the aubergine slices until soft.

5 Layer slices over the mince.

6 Break eggs into a bowl and stir in yogurt.

7 Pour over the moussaka, making sure sauce is spread to the edges.

8 Grate cheese and sprinkle on top of moussaka. Cook for 30–35 minutes until brown.

recipe tips
Moussaka is best served with a simple salad.
Not everyone likes the texture of grated vegetables, so you could just make this with meat and serve some vegetables as a side dish.

food fact
Moussaka is a savoury dish made of sliced aubergines and minced lamb. This dish originates in Greece and Turkey.

beef stir-fry

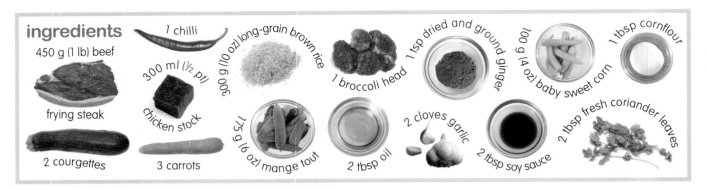

ingredients

450 g (1 lb) beef

frying steak

2 courgettes

1 chilli

300 ml (½ pt)

chicken stock

3 carrots

300 g (10 oz) long-grain brown rice

175 g (6 oz) mange tout

1 broccoli head

2 tbsp oil

1 tsp dried and ground ginger

2 cloves garlic

2 tbsp soy sauce

100 g (4 oz) baby sweet corn

1 tbsp cornflour

2 tbsp fresh coriander leaves

1 Cut the beef into long thin strips. Remove seeds and core from the chilli and chop.

2 Peel and thinly slice carrots. Cut broccoli into florets. Next, slice the courgettes 1 cm (½ in) thick and chop baby sweet corn in half.

3 Bring a saucepan of water to the boil and add carrots and broccoli to cook for 2 minutes. Remove the vegetables with a slotted spoon and keep to one side in a bowl. Add the rice to the saucepan and cook for 10–15 minutes until the rice is tender, but not mushy. Drain into colander.

4 Meanwhile, heat 1 tbsp oil in wok and fry carrots, broccoli and courgettes for 3 minutes.

5 Add baby corn and mange tout and cook for 2 minutes. Peel and crush garlic, add to wok and cook for 1 minute. Remove vegetables from wok and put in a large bowl.

6 Heat rest of oil in the wok, add beef and fry over a high heat for 5 minutes until browned. Add chopped chilli and ginger to the wok and cook for 1 minute.

7 In a small bowl, mix the soy sauce and cornflour together until smooth. Add to the wok with chicken stock and bring to the boil. Keep stirring for 1 minute.

8 Add coriander leaves and cooked vegetables to wok and heat for 1–2 minutes. Spoon rice onto serving plates and pile stir-fried meat and vegetables on top.

recipe idea
Use different meat or increase vegetables used to create a meat-free dish.

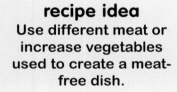

- **serves:** 4 ■ **preparation:** 15 minutes ■ **cooking:** 1 hour 40 minutes
- **oven temperature:** 190°C (375°F/Gas mark 5)

sticky chicken and sautéed potatoes

ingredients

1 onion

2 × 2 tbsp oil

2 tbsp tomato purée

2 tbsp Worcestershire sauce

3 tbsp clear honey

1 cloves garlic

Salt and Pepper

150 ml (¼ pt) chicken stock

2 tbsp soy sauce

8 chicken thighs

700 g (1¼ lb) potatoes

1 tbsp white-wine vinegar

1 Peel and chop onion. Peel and crush garlic. Heat oil in a saucepan and fry onion and garlic until onion starts to soften.

2 Add tomato purée, vinegar, honey, Worcestershire and soy sauce and chicken stock to the saucepan and bring to the boil. Lower the heat and simmer for 15–20 minutes. The sauce should thicken.

3 Preheat the oven. Arrange meat in a roasting tray and spoon sauce evenly over the meat. Cook for 30 minutes.

4 Use tongs to turn meat over and cook for a further 45 minutes, turning meat every 15 minutes and spooning sauce from the roasting tray over the top.

5 Meanwhile, peel potatoes and cut into 2.5 cm (1 in) cubes.

6 Boil a saucepan of water and cook potatoes for 3–5 minutes. Drain potatoes into a colander.

7 Put empty roasting tray into the oven to heat. Add oil and seasoning to potatoes and stir well. Carefully remove roasting tray from oven and spoon potatoes into it. Put back into the oven and cook for 30 minutes, until brown and crispy. Serve potatoes and meat together.

recipe idea
Serve with hot, buttered corn on the cob or a mixed salad.

main meals

■ **serves:** 4 ■ **preparation:** 30 minutes ■ **cooking:** 35–45 minutes
■ **oven temperature:** 190°C (375°F/Gas mark 5)

turkey parcels

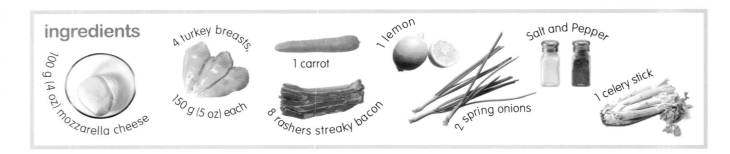

ingredients

100 g (4 oz) mozzarella cheese

4 turkey breasts, 150 g (5 oz) each

1 carrot

8 rashers streaky bacon

1 lemon

2 spring onions

Salt and Pepper

1 celery stick

1 Cut mozzarella into four pieces and put one piece on top of each turkey breast.

2 Wrap two bacon rashers around each one.

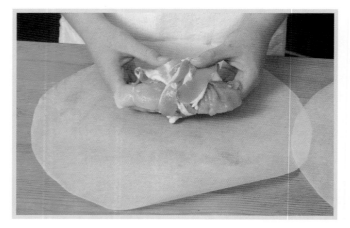

3 Cut four 30-cm (12-in) circles out of greaseproof paper and put a turkey breast just below the centre on each one.

4 Peel the carrot. Cut spring onions, carrot and celery into thin strips and arrange them on top of the turkey breasts.

You will also need a ruler

and greaseproof paper

5 Grate rind from lemon and squeeze the juice. Sprinkle rind and juice over meat and vegetables. Season with salt and pepper. Fold the paper over the meat and start on one side, twisting and folding the paper edges together.

6 Work your way around the semi-circle to seal the edges of the parcel. Fold each breast neatly. Put all the parcels in a roasting tray and cook for 35–45 minutes. Check the breasts are cooked right through.

7 Prepare and cook accompanying vegetables of your choice. Serve each parcel on a plate and let everyone open his or her own surprise!

recipe idea
Try different toppings, such as chopped tomatoes and mushrooms with a sweet chilli sauce.

oven-baked fish & chips

ingredients

2 tbsp olive oil

6 medium potatoes

225 g (8 oz) plain flour

225 g (8 oz) breadcrumbs
(see page 24)

4 thick pieces white fish

Salt and Pepper

225 g (8 oz) peas
(fresh, tinned or frozen)

4 eggs

1 Peel potatoes and cut into 1 cm (½ in) slices. Divide potatoes into stacks of two or three and cut into 1 cm (½ in) strips. Put into a bowl with 2 tbsp olive oil and mix well.

2 Grease a baking tray with a little oil. Cover baking tray with a single layer of chips. Bake chips for 45 minutes on top shelf of oven until golden brown. Turn them over with a spatula occasionally.

3 Meanwhile, put plain flour into one shallow dish with a little salt and pepper, breadcrumbs into another dish and break the eggs into a third dish. Whisk the eggs with a fork until they are well combined.

4 Take a fish piece and toss it in flour until covered all over. Next, dip it into egg until well coated and then straight into the breadcrumbs until completely covered.

5 Put the breadcrumbed fish onto a second greased baking tray, skin side down, and bake for 30–35 minutes until golden brown. Repeat with each fish piece. Cook peas according to instructions and serve.

recipe idea
Add 1 tbsp grated Parmesan to breadcrumbs to give a cheesy flavour.

recipe tip
When breadcrumbing fish pieces, it is easier to use one hand to dip fish into eggs and the other hand for flour and breadcrumbs. Otherwise, you could end up very messy!

vegetarian

cottage pie with special mash

ingredients

450 g (1 lb) potatoes

225 g (½ lb) carrots

1 onion

1 tbsp oil

225 g (½ lb) broccoli

450 g (1 lb) sweet potatoes

50 g (2 oz) butter

400 ml (14 fl oz) vegetable stock

225 g (½ lb) vegetarian mince

Salt and Pepper

50 g (2 oz) cheese

2 Add sweet potatoes and broccoli florets to boiling vegetables. Simmer for 8–10 minutes until all vegetables are soft.

3 Peel and chop onion. Heat oil in a clean saucepan, add chopped onion and cook for 3–4 minutes until soft.

1 Boil a saucepan of water. Peel and slice carrots, potatoes and sweet potatoes. Cut broccoli florets off. First boil carrots for 2–3 minutes, then add potatoes and cook for 10 minutes.

4 Add vegetarian mince and cook for 3 minutes, stirring often. Add vegetable stock, bring to the boil and then simmer for 10 minutes.

5 When the potatoes and other vegetables are cooked, drain them over a sink into a colander. Return to the saucepan and mash until smooth and lump free. Add butter and, seasoning. Stir well. Turn the grill to high.

6 When the mince is cooked, pour into an ovenproof dish. With a large spoon, put cooked potato on top of mince.

7 Smooth over with a fork. Grate cheese and sprinkle over the top of the mashed potato. Grill until golden brown.

recipe idea
Add a tin of baked beans, cooked green lentils or mixed cooked beans to the filling.

veggie burger

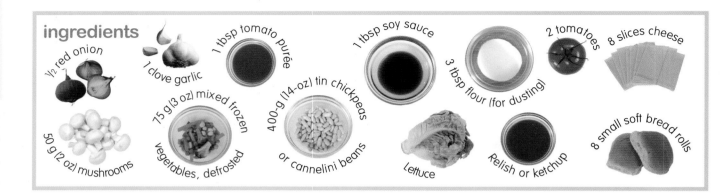

ingredients

½ red onion

1 clove garlic

50 g (2 oz) mushrooms

75 g (3 oz) mixed frozen vegetables, defrosted

1 tbsp tomato purée

400-g (14-oz) tin chickpeas or cannelini beans

1 tbsp soy sauce

3 tbsp flour (for dusting)

Lettuce

Relish or ketchup

2 tomatoes

8 slices cheese

8 small soft bread rolls

1 Peel and cut the onion into large chunks. Peel and crush the clove of garlic. Wipe mushrooms on a damp piece of kitchen roll.

2 Drain tin of chickpeas and put these ingredients into a food processor until finely chopped. If you don't have a processor, just chop the ingredients finely and mash with a potato-masher.

3 Add the defrosted vegetables, tomato purée and soy sauce and process until everything is just mixed.

4 Sprinkle some flour onto a plate. Spoon eight mounds of mixture onto the plate. Get your hands floury and shape each mound into a burger shape.

5 Heat 1 tbsp oil in a frying pan and fry four burgers at a time for 5 minutes on each side until browned. Repeat with the remaining burgers.

6 Slice tomatoes thinly. Cut bread rolls in half and put a layer of lettuce on each roll base and a burger on top. Next, add grated/sliced cheese and top with sliced tomato. Spread burger relish or ketchup over the roll top and put onto the burger. Serve.

recipe idea
Cook some potato waffles and put one on top of each burger with a poached egg (see page 23).

broccoli & egg macaroni cheese

ingredients

225 g (8 oz) wholewheat or plain macaroni

4 eggs

1 broccoli head

600 ml (1 pt) milk

100 g (4 oz) plain flour

100 g (4 oz) butter

1 tsp mustard

Salt and Pepper

350 g (12 oz) cheese

1 Fill a saucepan two-thirds full of water and bring to the boil. Add the macaroni and boil for 8–10 minutes. When cooked, drain in a colander over the sink and rest colander on a plate.

2 Meanwhile, bring another saucepan of water to the boil and boil eggs for 5 minutes. Remove eggs from water with a slotted spoon and put in a bowl of cold water. Keep the saucepan of water boiling

3 Cut each broccoli floret off and put into the boiling water. Cook for 5 minutes, then drain into a colander.

4 Put milk, flour and butter into a saucepan and gently bring to the boil. With a wooden spoon, keep stirring the mixture until the sauce is thick and smooth. Season with salt and pepper, add mustard and stir sauce for 2–3 minutes.

5 Grate cheese and add half to the white sauce. Stir until it has melted.

6 Peel and cut the boiled eggs into quarters.

7 Stir the chopped eggs, drained macaroni and broccoli into cheese sauce.

8 Pour whole mixture into an ovenproof dish and sprinkle the remaining grated cheese over the top.

9 Put under the grill until golden brown and bubbling.

recipe tip
Chop a leek and some mushrooms and add to step 6 for a tasty alternative. Serve with salad.

vegetarian

mediterranean vegetable cobbler

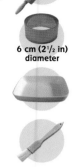

6 cm (2½ in) diameter

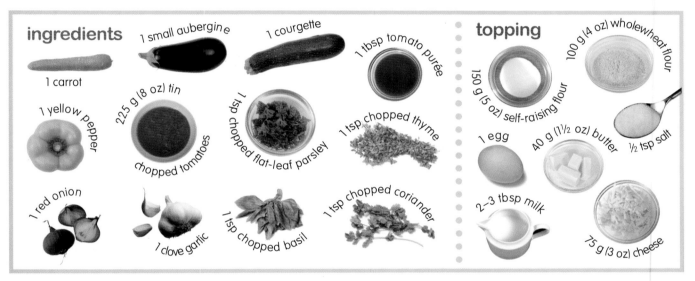

ingredients

1 carrot

1 small aubergine

1 courgette

1 tbsp tomato purée

1 yellow pepper

225 g (8 oz) tin chopped tomatoes

1 tsp chopped flat-leaf parsley

1 tsp chopped thyme

1 red onion

1 clove garlic

1 tsp chopped basil

1 tsp chopped coriander

topping

150 g (5 oz) self-raising flour

100 g (4 oz) wholewheat flour

1 egg

40 g (1½ oz) butter

½ tsp salt

2–3 tbsp milk

75 g (3 oz) cheese

1 Trim ends off aubergine and courgette, cut into 1 cm (½ in) slices and dice. Peel and chop onion. Deseed and chop pepper. Chop carrot.

2 Put prepared vegetables, tomatoes and chopped herbs into a saucepan. Peel and crush garlic and add to saucepan. Bring to the boil and simmer for 20 minutes. Add tomato purée and cook for 5 minutes.

3 To make scone topping, sift the flours and salt into a mixing bowl (add the bran collected in the sieve to mixing bowl). Add butter and rub in using your fingertips until the mixture resembles breadcrumbs. Grate cheese into mixture and stir.

4 In a small bowl, mix egg with 2 tbsp milk. Add this to the mixing bowl and use your clean hands to make soft dough. If bits of dry mixture are left in the bowl, add extra milk so that the bowl is left clean.

5 Sprinkle some flour onto the worktop, roll dough out until 1 cm (½ in) thick and cut out rounds using a cutter.

6 Reroll leftover dough until all is used up.

7 Pour vegetable mixture into ovenproof dish and layer scones on top.

8 Brush scones with a little milk and put into the oven for 20 minutes until brown.

recipe idea
Pastry can be used to cover the filling if preferred.

vegetables with cheesy dumplings

1 Peel swede and cut into chunks.

2 Peel and slice parsnips, carrots and onion. Chop pieces if too big. Slice celery. Deseed and chop pepper.

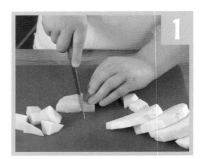

3 In a saucepan, melt margarine and oil, add all prepared vegetables and cook for 5 minutes.

4 Add vegetable stock and herbs. Bring to the boil and simmer for 20 minutes until the vegetables are soft.

ingredients

225 g (½ lb) parsnips

4 carrots

1 onion

1 red pepper

25 g (1 oz) margarine

450 g (1 lb) swede

3 celery stalks

1 tbsp oil

1.2 l (2 pt) vegetable stock

1 tsp mixed herbs and ½ tsp dried rosemary

225 g (½ lb) cauliflower florets

225 g (½ lb) broccoli florets

ingredients - Dumplings

25 g (1 oz) Parmesan cheese

50 g (2 oz) cheese

¼ tsp salt

100 g (4 oz) self-raising flour

Salt and Pepper

50 g (2 oz) vegetable suet

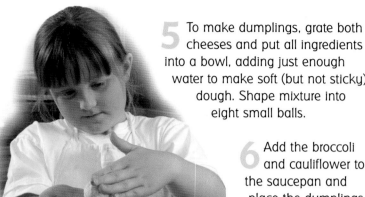

5 To make dumplings, grate both cheeses and put all ingredients into a bowl, adding just enough water to make soft (but not sticky) dough. Shape mixture into eight small balls.

6 Add the broccoli and cauliflower to the saucepan and place the dumplings around the top. Cover the saucepan with a lid and simmer for 20 minutes until the dumplings are cooked.

recipe idea
Vary the ingredients using vegetables in season or your favourites.

cheesy broccoli & cauliflower crumble

1 Put a saucepan of water on to boil. Cut broccoli and cauliflower into florets. Boil for 5 minutes until just tender. Drain in a colander and transfer to an ovenproof dish. Add sweetcorn

ingredients

- 400 g (14 oz) broccoli
- 50 g (2 oz) butter
- 175 g (6 oz) mature cheese
- 100g (4oz) sweetcorn (cooked)
- 475 ml (16 fl oz) milk
- Salt and Pepper
- 400g (14oz) cauliflower
- 50 g (2 oz) plain flour
- 1 tsp mustard

ingredients - Topping

- 50 g (2 oz) breadcrumbs
- 25 g (1 oz) butter
- 50 g (2 oz) oats

2 Melt butter in a saucepan, stir in the flour and cook for 1 minute. Gradually stir in milk, stirring all the time until the sauce boils. Whisk until the sauce is thick and smooth.

3 Grate cheese and add half to the sauce with mustard, salt and pepper. Stir well until the cheese has melted.

4 Preheat grill. Prepare and start cooking any vegetables you wish to serve. To make the topping, melt the butter in a saucepan, stir in the breadcrumbs and add the remaining grated cheese and oats.

5 Sprinkle topping over cheesy vegetables and grill for 5 minutes, until crumble is brown and sauce is bubbling.

recipe idea
Try adding cooked cauliflower florets or sliced boiled egg.

cheesy sausage hot dogs

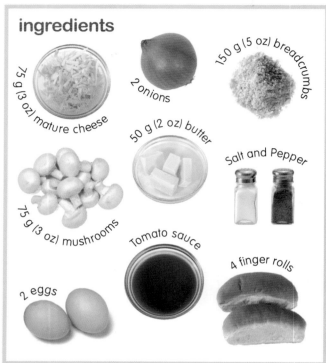

ingredients

75 g (3 oz) mature cheese

2 onions

150 g (5 oz) breadcrumbs

50 g (2 oz) butter

Salt and Pepper

75 g (3 oz) mushrooms

Tomato sauce

4 finger rolls

2 eggs

1 Grate cheese and put into a mixing bowl. Peel and finely chop mushrooms and then stir into cheese, along with 75 g (3 oz) breadcrumbs and a sprinkle of salt and pepper.

2 Separate eggs into cups and add the egg yolks to the mixing bowl. Mix well.

3 With wet hands, shape the mixture into eight sausages. Put the egg white into one shallow dish and whisk lightly with a fork. In the other dish, put the remaining breadcrumbs.

4 Roll each sausage in egg white and then in breadcrumbs.

5 Preheat grill and cook sausages for 10–15 minutes, turning regularly.

6 Peel and slice the onions. Melt butter in a frying pan and cook the onion rings until soft and starting to brown.

7 When sausages and onions are cooked, slice down the centre of each finger roll, put in a sausage (or two!) and top with cooked onion and tomato sauce.

recipe idea
Serve sausages with mashed potato and baked beans or vegetables.

special
diet

egg & tomatoes on toasted ciabatta

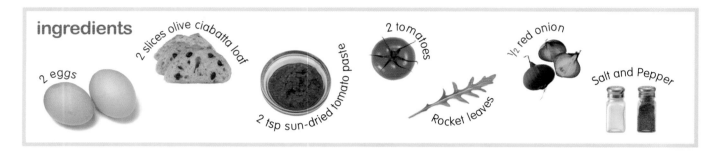

ingredients

2 eggs

2 slices olive ciabatta loaf

2 tsp sun-dried tomato paste

2 tomatoes

Rocket leaves

½ red onion

Salt and Pepper

1 Half fill a saucepan with water and bring to the boil. Break an egg into a cup.

2 Gently slide egg into boiling water. Repeat with second egg. Remove saucepan from heat and keep in a warm place for 8–10 minutes.

3 Lightly toast each slice of ciabatta. Spread a dessertspoon of sun-dried tomato paste onto each slice of bread. Put grill on high.

4 Slice tomatoes thinly and place on top of bread. Grill for 3–4 minutes until tomatoes are light brown.

5 Quickly arrange rocket leaves on side of each plate. Peel and thinly slice red onion and sprinkle on top of rocket leaves.

6 Sprinkle toasted tomatoes lightly with salt and pepper. Put toast onto serving plate. Remove egg from saucepan with a slotted spoon and put on top of toast. Sprinkle with salt and pepper.

chicken tacos

ingredients

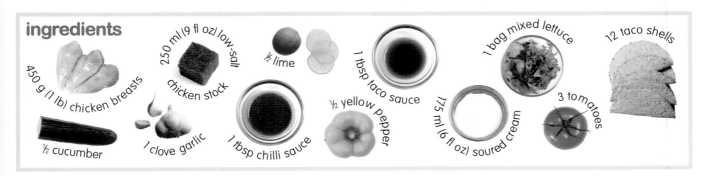

450 g (1 lb) chicken breasts

250 ml (9 fl oz) low-salt chicken stock

½ cucumber

1 clove garlic

½ lime

1 tbsp chilli sauce

½ yellow pepper

1 tbsp taco sauce

175 ml (6 fl oz) soured cream

1 bag mixed lettuce

3 tomatoes

12 taco shells

1 Cut chicken breasts in half and place in a saucepan with water, stock cube and chilli sauce.

2 Peel and crush clove of garlic and add to saucepan. Bring ingredients to the boil. Reduce the heat so liquid in saucepan simmers for 10 minutes. Remove from the heat and leave for 15 minutes.

3 Meanwhile, in a bowl, squeeze the lime juice with taco sauce.

4 Slice tomatoes, cucumber and pepper.

5 Add to the lettuce and salad ingredients in a separate bowl.

6 Slice cooled chicken thinly and mix into taco and lime sauce.

7 Warm taco shells according to packet instructions.

8 In each taco shell, sprinkle some mixed salad, followed by chicken and topped with a spoonful of soured cream.

recipe idea
Any lean meat can be used in this recipe, but remember to use appropriate stock cubes, e.g., beef stock cubes for beef, pork for pork and so on.

special diet – diabetic

wholemeal fruity scones

1 Rub margarine or butter onto baking tray, spreading to all sides to make sure scones don't stick to the tray.

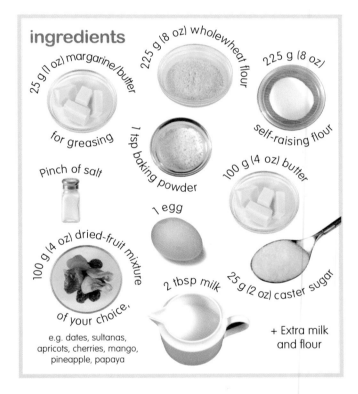

ingredients

25 g (1 oz) margarine/butter
for greasing

225 g (8 oz) wholewheat flour

225 g (8 oz) self-raising flour

1 tsp baking powder

Pinch of salt

100 g (4 oz) butter

1 egg

100 g (4 oz) dried-fruit mixture of your choice,
e.g. dates, sultanas, apricots, cherries, mango, pineapple, papaya

2 tbsp milk

25 g (2 oz) caster sugar

+ Extra milk and flour

6 cm (2½ in) diameter

2 In a mixing bowl, sift the flours, emptying the bran left in the sieve back into the mixing bowl. Add the baking powder and a pinch of salt. Add butter and rub in until mixture resembles breadcrumbs.

3 Chop dried fruit and add to bowl with sugar. Break egg into a small bowl and whisk with a fork.

4 Make a well in the centre of mixture and pour in egg and 2 tbsp milk.

5 Use a fork to mix the ingredients together roughly. If dough is dry and does not stick together, add a little more milk. Gently knead with your hands until dough is smooth.

6 Dust the worktop with a little self-raising flour and lift mixture onto it. Gently roll dough to 2 cm (³/₄ in) thick.

7 Use a cutter to cut out scones. Place onto baking sheet, making sure there is a gap of 2.5-5 cm (1-2 in) between scones. Reroll dough left and cut again until all the dough has been used up.

8 Pour a little milk into a cup and use a pastry brush to glaze the tops of each scone. Bake on a high shelf for 15-20 minutes until lightly browned. Cool on the tray for 5 minutes, then transfer scones to a wire cooling rack.

recipe tip
Serve while warm,
cut in half and
spread with butter.

plum crumble

ingredients

50 g (4 oz) demerara sugar

2 tbsp water

900 g (2 lb) plums

ingredients - Topping

50 g (4 oz) wholewheat flour

75 g (3 oz) butter

50 g (4 oz) porridge oats

50 g (4 oz) demerara sugar

1 Place plums in a colander and rinse under running water. Cut each in half around the stone. Remove stone and place plum halves in a saucepan with sugar and water.

2 Bring to the boil, reduce heat and cook fruit gently for 15 minutes until plums are soft. Stir occasionally. Meanwhile, in a mixing bowl, sift flour, add butter and rub in gently using your fingertips.

3 When mixture resembles breadcrumbs, add oats and sugar and stir ingredients together with a spoon.

5 Use a fork to even the topping gently. Cook for 30–40 minutes until the top is a light-brown colour.

4 When plums are cooked, very carefully spoon fruit into a pie dish. Sprinkle topping onto fruit.

recipe tip
Other crumble filling ideas are apple, blackcurrant, soaked dried fruit, rhubarb, gooseberry, summer fruits or a combination of fruits. Muesli or nuts can be added to the crumble topping for variation.

- **serves:** 4 ■ **preparation:** 20 minutes ■ **cooking:** 50–60 minutes
- **oven temperature:** 200°C (400°F/Gas mark 6)

maple-syrup turkey

1 Butter the inside of an ovenproof dish and put turkey breasts in the dish.

ingredients

Butter for greasing
4 turkey breasts
½ red pepper
40 g (1½ oz) butter
½ green pepper
100 g (4 oz) maple syrup
1 lemon
Baby vegetables to serve
700g (1½ lb) new potatoes
Salt and Pepper

2 Deseed and chop peppers into chunks, sprinkle over turkey. Grate 1 tsp rind from lemon, cut lemon in half, squeeze 1 tbsp juice into a small bowl and add rind.

3 Melt butter in a small saucepan. Mix maple syrup and melted butter in the bowl with lemon juice and rind. Add a sprinkle of salt and pepper and pour over turkey.

4 Bake in the oven for 50-60 minutes. Every 15 minutes, carefully remove the dish and baste. Make sure the syrup does not splash you. If the sauce starts to dry up, add extra maple syrup. At the end, the sauce will be thick and sticky.

5 Put two saucepans of water on to boil. Scrub new potatoes in clean water with a nailbrush to remove dirt. Boil potatoes 15-20 minutes before the end of the turkey cooking time. Check potatoes are soft when a knife is inserted, then drain into a colander over a sink.

6 Put the baby vegetables into the other saucepan to cook for 5-7 minutes before the end of the potato/turkey cooking time, drain into a colander over a sink and serve with the cooked potatoes and turkey.

summer-fruit pancakes

1 Break an egg into a small bowl and add milk. Melt the butter/margarine in a small saucepan and pour it into the small bowl.

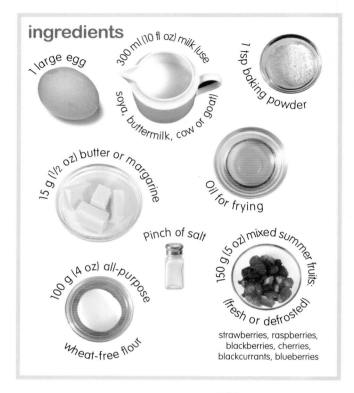

ingredients

1 large egg

300 ml (10 fl oz) milk (use soya, buttermilk, cow or goat)

1 tsp baking powder

15 g (½ oz) butter or margarine

Oil for frying

Pinch of salt

100 g (4 oz) all-purpose wheat-free flour

150 g (5 oz) mixed summer fruits: (fresh or defrosted)

strawberries, raspberries, blackberries, cherries, blackcurrants, blueberries

2 Whisk well.

3 Sift the flour, baking powder and salt into a mixing bowl and then stir in the milk mixture from step 1.

4 Put the mixture in the fridge for 30 minutes. Heat 1 tbsp oil in a small omelette pan and spoon a ladle of mixture into the pan. Sprinkle some summer fruits on the top.

5 Cook pancakes for 2–3 minutes, turn pancakes over with a spatula and cook for a further 1–1½ minutes. Put cooked pancakes on a plate to keep warm in a heated oven until all the mixture is cooked.

6 Repeat steps 4 and 5 until all the mixture has been used. Put a piece of baking parchment between each pancake to prevent them sticking together.

recipe idea
Serve with ice cream, thick Greek yogurt or a drizzle of maple syrup.

special diet – wheat free

- **makes:** 20 - **preparation:** 25 minutes - **cooking:** 15 minutes
- **oven temperature:** 180°C (350°F/Gas mark 4)

date cookies

ingredients

50 g (2 oz) porridge oats

75 g (3 oz) rice flour

½ tsp bicarbonate of soda

75 g (3 oz) margarine or butter

250 g (9 oz) dried dates

100 g (4 oz) sultanas

2 eggs

100 g (4 oz) eating apple

1 Rub together oats, rice flour, bicarbonate of soda and margarine/butter in a mixing bowl until everything is combined and crumbly.

2 Chop dates into chunks and add to bowl, along with sultanas. Remove apple core and chop apple into small chunks. Add to bowl and mix ingredients well.

3 Break eggs into a cup, pour into mixing bowl and mix until well combined.

4 Line baking tray with baking parchment and put dessertspoons of mixture in rows that are 2.5 cm (1 in) apart.

5 Pat a fork gently on each cookie to flatten slightly. Bake on the centre shelf of the oven for 15 minutes.

6 Remove cookies from baking tray with a spatula and cool on a wire rack.

recipe idea
Try other dried fruits, such as mango, pineapple, banana, apricots, cranberries and apple.

■ **serves:** 8 ■ **preparation:** 15 minutes
■ **cooking and chilling timing:** 2 hours 10 minutes

white-chocolate & cherry polenta cake

1 Grease a cake tin with a little oil. Pour water into a saucepan and bring to the boil. Break 200 g (7 oz) of the chocolate into chunks and cut cherries in half.

ingredients

750 ml (1¼ pt) water

350 g (1] oz) white chocolate

175 g (6 oz) cherries

½ tsp baking powder

175 g (6 oz) instant polenta

6 oz glacé cherries & some for decoration

2 Add polenta and baking powder to water, then mash as quickly as possible.

3 Add broken chocolate and cherries to saucepan and stir in with a wooden spoon until chocolate has melted and everything is well mixed.

4 Pour mixture into loose-bottomed tin and level top of cake with the back of a spoon. Leave to cool for 10 minutes.

5 Grate remaining chocolate and sprinkle on top of cake.

6 Cut glacé cherries in half and place around edges of cake.

7 Put cake in fridge to chill for a minimum of 2 hours.

recipe idea
Use milk or dark chocolate if preferred. Instead of cherries, try chocolate chips or other dried fruits.

wholemeal pitta dog

ingredients

8 sausages

4 wholemeal pitta breads

8 tbsp guacamole

Mixed salad

(vegetarian, vegan, beef or pork)

1 Grill sausages under medium heat. Turn sausages regularly with a fork to brown evenly. Leave to cool for a few minutes.

2 Heat pitta bread according to packet instructions. Leave to cool for a few minutes. Slice a slit along the top of each pitta bread.

3 Spoon 2 tbsp guacamole inside each pitta and spread evenly with a knife.

4 Slice sausages lengthwise.

5 Divide between the pittas.

6 Top sausages with mixed salad leaves and serve.

- **serves:** 6　■ **preparation:** 30 minutes　■ **cooking:** 35–40 minutes
- **oven temperature:** 200°C (400°F/Gas mark 6)

carrot and pea flan

ingredients

175 g (6 oz) self-raising flour

175 g (6 oz) wholewheat flour

Cold water

900 g (2 lb) carrots

175 g (6 oz) dairy-free vegetable margarine

1 clove garlic

1 red onion

4 tbsp olive oil

50 g (2 oz) fresh or defrosted frozen peas

4 eggs

4 tsp chopped parsley

Salt and Pepper

150 ml (¼ pt) soya milk

1 To make pastry, sift the flours and a little salt into a mixing bowl (put bits left in the sieve into the bowl, too). Cut margarine into small cubes and add to flour. Use your fingertips lightly to rub the fat into the flour.

2 When the mixture looks crumbly, sprinkle about 2 tablespoons of water over the mixture and use your hands to mix the ingredients into smooth dough. Add more water as needed.

3 The bowl should be clean, with no bits of flour left behind. Wrap the pastry in plastic wrap and rest in the fridge for 30 minutes.

4 Peel carrots and grate them. Peel onion and chop. Peel garlic and crush with garlic-crusher.

5 Heat oil in a frying pan and cook grated carrots, chopped onion and crushed garlic gently for 10 minutes with a lid on the pan. Stir in peas and chopped parsley and put pan to one side to cool.

6 Sift a little self-raising flour on the worktop and roll pastry out on it. Roll one direction a few times, turn pastry 45 degrees and roll a few times, turn pastry over and repeat until you have a circle of pastry large enough to fit the flan dish and cover the sides.

7 Grease flan dish with a little margarine and line flan dish with pastry.

8 Evenly arrange mixture in the pastry case.

9 Measure milk in a jug, add eggs and seasoning and pour over filling. Then put in the oven for 25–30 minutes.

10 Slice and serve.

recipe idea
Serve with new potatoes and side salad or coleslaw.

You will also need a large plastic bag, with seal

chicken nuggets with tomato sauce

1 Start with the sauce. Boil a kettle of water. Put tomatoes in a bowl and cover with boiling water. Leave for 1–2 minutes.

ingredients

450 g (1 lb) ripe tomatoes

1 small onion

1 clove garlic

1 tsp tomato purée

1 tsp basil (fresh or dried)

1 tbsp olive oil

5 tbsp dairy-free margarine

Salt and Pepper

3 tsp Worcestershire sauce

900 g (2 lb) chicken breasts

200 g (7 oz) plain crisps

2 Remove with a slotted spoon. When cooled, slide skins off and discard.

3 Chop flesh into small chunks.

4 Peel and chop onion. Peel and crush clove of garlic. Heat olive oil in a saucepan and gently cook onion and garlic for 5 minutes with a lid on, but stir often.

5 Add chopped tomatoes, tomato purée, basil and salt and pepper. Stir well and cover pan with a lid. Simmer for 10 minutes. Remove lid, stir ingredients and leave uncovered to simmer for another 10 minutes.

6 Preheat the oven. In a small saucepan, melt the margarine. Pour into a large bowl and add Worcestershire sauce. Cut chicken into 2.5 cm (1 in) chunks. Add them to the margarine and stir well to coat in melted margarine.

7 Seal crisps in a plastic bag and then crush with a rolling pin.

8 Use a slotted spoon to add chicken pieces to the bag.

9 Shake well to coat evenly. Put chicken nuggets onto baking tray and bake for 10 minutes. Test a chicken nugget to make sure it is cooked through.

recipe idea
The tomato sauce can be served warm or cold, as it is or blended smooth using a hand blender.

181

■ **makes:** 1 loaf ■ **preparation:** 15-20 minutes ■ **cooking:** 1-1½ hours
■ **oven temperature:** 170°C (325°F/Gas mark 3)

banana bread

ingredients

100 g (4 oz) dairy-free margarine & extra for greasing

2 eggs

2 tbsp soya milk

225 g (8 oz) plain white flour

2 tsp baking powder

1 lemon

1 orange

50 g (2 oz) sultanas

4 medium bananas

2 tbsp coconut milk

1 Preheat oven. Line base of tin with greaseproof paper, grease tin. Put margarine and eggs in a mixing bowl and beat eggs with a wooden spoon.

2 Add soya milk and whisk until the mixture is pale and fluffy.

3 Sift flour and baking powder into the bowl. Grate orange and lemon rind and add to the bowl with the sultanas.

4 In a separate bowl, mash the bananas to a pulp with a fork. Then add to the mixture, along with coconut milk.

5 Spoon the mixture into a prepared loaf tin and bake for 1 hour. Check with a skewer to see if the bread is cooked. If not, return to oven for 15–30 minutes.

6 Leave bread in tin for 5 minutes. Using oven gloves to protect your hands, place cooling rack on top of loaf tin and invert so that the banana bread slides out easily. Leave to cool.

desserts

fresh fruit fools

1 Rinse the fruit under running water in a colander and hull by pulling out the stalk.

2 Put fruit into liquidiser with sugar and blitz until smooth.

ingredients

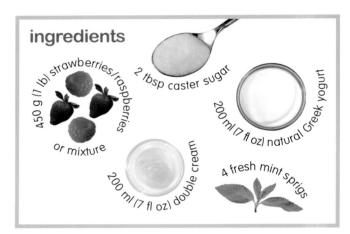

450 g (1 lb) strawberries/raspberries or mixture

2 tbsp caster sugar

200 ml (7 fl oz) natural Greek yogurt

200 ml (7 fl oz) double cream

4 fresh mint sprigs

4 Add two-thirds of the puréed strawberry mixture to mixing bowl. Stir ingredients together a few times until mixture looks marbled. There should be red veins running through the cream/yogurt.

3 In a mixing bowl, whip cream until stiff with an electric handwhisk (do not overbeat). Gently stir Greek yogurt into whipped cream until well combined.

5 Spoon a tablespoon of strawberry purée into the bottom of each glass serving bowl. Spoon yogurt mixture into the glass, leaving 2.5 cm (1/2 in) space at top of glass.

6 Top with a spoonful of strawberry mixture and a sprig of mint just before serving.

recipe idea
Use other fruits or a mixture, for example, banana, apricot, summer fruits, rhubarb, gooseberry, peach or nectarine.

recipe tip
This recipe is even more delicious if left overnight in the fridge to chill.

■ **serves:** 6 ■ **preparation:** 20 minutes ■ **cooking:** 45 minutes
■ **oven temperature:** 180°C (350°F/Gas mark 4)

fruit flapjack

ingredients

125 g (4½ oz) butter

100 g (4 oz) soft dark-brown sugar

50 g (2 oz) sultanas

175 g (6 oz) porridge oats

100 g (4 oz) black seedless grapes

100 g (4 oz) large strawberries

425 g (15 oz) tin apricots halves in fruit juice

Squeeze of lemon juice

2 kiwi fruits

2 tsp cornflour

1 Preheat oven. Put butter into a saucepan and gently melt it. Add sugar, oats and sultanas and stir well.

2 Grease a flan dish with butter. Pat mixture firmly into the dish. Bake in the oven for 20 minutes.

3 Meanwhile, prepare the fruit. Remove stalks from strawberries and slice. Cut grapes in half lengthways. Peel and slice kiwi fruits.

4 When base is cooked, leave to cool slightly so that the dish is warm, but not hot. Arrange strawberry slices across the centre of the base. The strawberry slices should overlap.

5 Place a row of grapes either side of the strawberries. Drain juice from apricot tin into a small bowl and keep to one side. Place a row of apricots down either side of the grapes. Overlap slices of kiwi fruit either side of the apricots.

6 Mix 3 tbsp of reserved juice, cornflour and a squeeze of lemon juice. Pour into a small saucepan and bring gently to the boil. Stir well, and when sauce is thick and glossy, glaze the fruit with a pastry brush or the back of a spoon. Serve warm or cold.

recipe idea
For a quick dessert, use ready-made flapjack and vary the fruit used, depending on what is in your fruit bowl.

■ **makes:** 12 dumplings ■ **preparation:** 30 minutes ■ **cooking:** 15–20 minutes
■ **oven temperature:** 220°C (425°F/Gas mark 7)

banana dumplings

1 Preheat oven and brush baking sheet with water. Sprinkle a little flour on the work surface to prevent pastry sticking.

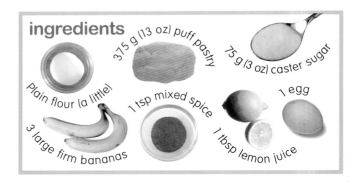

ingredients

375 g (13 oz) puff pastry

75 g (3 oz) caster sugar

Plain flour (a little)

1 tsp mixed spice

1 egg

3 large firm bananas

1 tbsp lemon juice

2 Roll out pastry into a 51 x 38 cm (20 x 15 in) rectangle. Trim edges straight and leave to rest for 5–10 minutes.

3 Cut pastry into 12 squares, each measuring 12.5 cm (5 in). Cut bananas into quarters crossways and put into a bowl.

4 Sprinkle lemon juice onto bananas and stir gently with a spoon.

5 Place one piece of banana diagonally in the centre of each square. In a separate bowl, mix sugar and spice together and sprinkle 1 tsp of mixture over each banana piece.

6 Break egg into a cup and whisk lightly with a fork. Brush edges of each pastry square with beaten egg and then lift two opposite corners and stick together.

7 Lift the other two corners and stick together. Stick open seams together.

8 Brush each dumpling with egg, sprinkle with remaining sugar and bake for 15–20 minutes, until golden brown.

recipe idea
Serve with ice cream, whipped cream, clotted cream or custard.

serves: 4–5 people ■ **preparation:** 20–25 minutes ■ **cooking:** 20 minutes

chocolate fondue

ingredients

200 g (7 oz) sweet good-quality chocolate

8 tbsp condensed milk

300 ml (½ pt) double cream

1 tsp vanilla extract

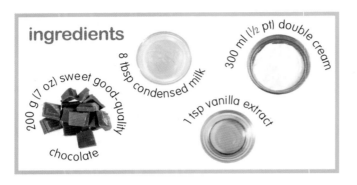

1 Prepare the fruit that you want to use as dippers (see right). Wash fruit and remove stalks, skin or stones. Chop into bite-size pieces.

2 Arrange dippers on a large plate or platter.

3 If using bananas and apples, give them a squirt with lemon juice to prevent them turning brown.

food fact
When the cut surface of some fruit and vegetables comes into contact with the air, it can discolour and turn brown. Acid from lemon juice prevents this.

4 To make fondue, break chocolate into pieces and put into a saucepan. Add cream and condensed milk. Melt over a low heat, stirring occasionally until sauce is smooth. Add vanilla extract and stir again.

recipe idea
For a white-chocolate fondue, use 175 g (6 oz) white chocolate, 75 g (3 oz) honey and 4 tbsp evaporated milk. Break chocolate into pieces and place in a saucepan. Add honey and melt over a low heat. Stir occasionally. Add evaporated milk and stir until smooth. Pour into a fondue pot or small bowls and serve.

5 Pour sauce into a fondue pot or small bowls. Use fondue forks or toothpicks to 'spear' the fruit and sweets. Dip into chocolate and enjoy!

dipper ideas
Banana, pineapple chunks, orange segments, kiwi fruit, apples, cherries, marshmallows, biscuits.

easy strawberry trifle

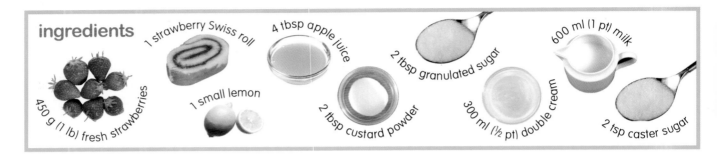

ingredients

450 g (1 lb) fresh strawberries

1 strawberry Swiss roll

1 small lemon

4 tbsp apple juice

2 tbsp custard powder

2 tbsp granulated sugar

300 ml (½ pt) double cream

600 ml (1 pt) milk

2 tsp caster sugar

1 Pull out the strawberry stalks; use a small knife if you need to. Cut most of the strawberries in half, but save four for decoration. Put the chopped pieces into a large glass serving bowl.

2 Use a serrated knife to slice the Swiss roll into 2.5 cm (1 in) slices.

3 Put the cake on top of the strawberries.

4 Sprinkle with apple juice. Mix gently. Cover the bowl with plastic wrap and put in the fridge.

5 Put custard powder and 1 tbsp granulated sugar into a cup and add 2 tbsp milk. Mix well to make a smooth paste.

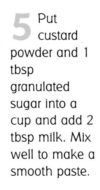

6 Heat milk gently in saucepan and, when almost boiling, remove pan from heat and stir in custard-powder paste. Stir well and return to a low heat until the custard starts to boil. Stir continually. Reduce heat so custard simmers for 2–3 minutes. Remove from heat, sprinkle remaining granulated sugar over the custard surface and cool for 30 minutes.

7 Meanwhile, grate rind from lemon and put in a mixing bowl.

8 Add caster sugar and cream and whisk until cream becomes stiff. Do not overbeat or you will end up with butter!

9 Remove strawberry and sponge bowl from fridge and pour over custard. Smooth flat with a spoon if needed. Spread cream mixture over custard.

10 Decorate with reserved strawberries and put back into the fridge to cool for 1–2 hours, or until trifle is needed.

recipe idea
Use tinned fruit, or vary fruit used. The trifle can be made in individual serving bowls if preferred.

recipe tip
Sprinkling some sugar over the surface of cooling custard prevents a skin from forming.

You will also need sticky tape,

a tray (plastic or metal)

and paper and pens or pencils

orange jelly boats

ingredients

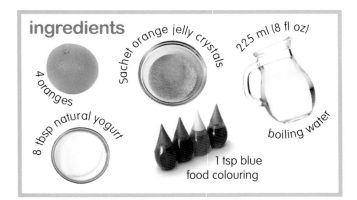

4 oranges

Sachet orange jelly crystals

225 ml (8 fl oz)

8 tbsp natural yogurt

1 tsp blue food colouring

boiling water

1 Cut oranges in half horizontally. Rest sieve over mixing bowl. Use dessertspoon to scoop out orange flesh and put into sieve.

2 Squeeze orange juice out of flesh by pushing it into sieve with the back of a spoon.

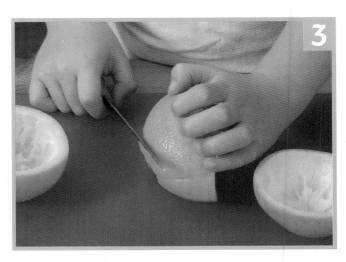

3 Put orange shells onto tray. If they roll around, just cut a thin slice off the bottom of each orange half.

4 Dissolve jelly crystals in 235 ml (8 fl oz) boiling water and add juice from oranges.

5 Spoon jelly into orange shells and chill in the fridge until set.

6 To decorate, cut out sail and flag shapes from paper and decorate with coloured pencils. Stick flags and sails to cocktail sticks with sticky tape.

7 In a mixing bowl, combine yogurt with food colouring and cover serving plates with a thin layer of blue 'sea'.

8 Put set jelly boats onto sea and decorate with colourful flags and sails.

recipe tip
Remove sails/
flags before
eating.

raspberry jelly cream

ingredients

150 ml (¼ pt)
boiling water

125 g (4½ oz) raspberry jelly

175 g (6 oz) evaporated milk

300 ml (½ pt) fruit juice
(apple or raspberry)

400 g (14 oz) raspberries
Fresh or tinned raspberries
in natural juice
Plus some to serve

1 Break jelly into pieces and put into a measuring jug. Pour over boiling water and stir until jelly dissolves. Add fruit juice to top total jug content to 450 ml (¾ pt). Pour jelly into bowl and freeze for 20 minutes until almost set.

2 In a bowl, whisk evaporated milk until thick.

3 When jelly is almost set, remove from freezer and fold in milk and fresh raspberries. Make sure the ingredients are well combined.

4 Spoon mixture into a jelly mould and chill for 1½ hours, until set.

5 To remove from mould, fill a large bowl with hot water. Dip mould into hot water for a count of ten. Loosen edges with a knife. Put a plate over the top of mould and quickly turn mould upside down. Serve with extra raspberries.

recipe idea
Vary fruit, for example, use strawberries, rhubarb or nectarines.

recipe tip
Rinse inside of mould with water and shake out excess before use – this should help removal later.

lemon sponge dessert

ingredients

3 lemons

+ 1 extra lemon for decoration

400 g (14 oz) tin condensed milk

1 packet trifle sponges

3 egg whites

200 ml (7 fl oz) double cream

3 Whisk egg whites until stiff.

1 Line a loaf tin with foil, making sure that there is 12.5 cm (5 in) extra foil all around to fold over and cover the dessert when prepared.

2 Squeeze juice and grate rind of three lemons and put into a bowl. Add condensed milk.

4 Fold into lemon mixture.

5 Line base of loaf tin with a layer of trifle sponges and top with a layer of lemon mixture. Repeat until loaf tin is full and lemon mixture is used up. Wrap foil over the sponge dessert and chill in the fridge overnight.

6 To serve, whisk cream until thick. Remove foil pack from loaf tin and peel foil from chilled lemon sponge. Put onto a serving plate. Use a palette knife to cover sponge with cream and decorate with a few slices of lemon and a little grated lemon rind.

■ **serves:** 6 ■ **preparation:** 40 minutes ■ **cooking:** 1 hour
■ **oven temperature:** 140°C (275°F/Gas mark 1)

fruit pavlova

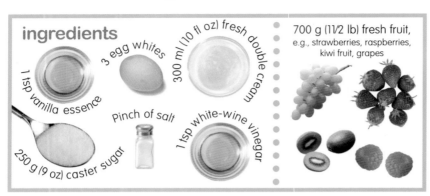

ingredients

1 tsp vanilla essence

3 egg whites

300 ml (10 fl oz) fresh double cream

700 g (1½ lb) fresh fruit, e.g., strawberries, raspberries, kiwi fruit, grapes

250 g (9 oz) caster sugar

Pinch of salt

1 tsp white-wine vinegar

1 Draw a circle on non-stick paper by drawing around a plate/cake tin (about 23 cm/9 in). Do not cut out the circle, but put the sheet of paper on a baking tray.

2 Put egg whites and salt into a mixing bowl and whisk until very stiff. Sift quarter of the sugar into bowl and whisk. Add another quarter and whisk again. Repeat until all of the sugar has been added. Beat until mixture forms stiff peaks when whisk is removed.

3 Add vanilla essence and vinegar and whisk until mixed in. Use a palette knife to spread mixture over paper circle and bake in oven for 1 hour until firm.

4 Leave to cool completely and remove paper carefully. Put onto a serving plate.

5 In a clean bowl, whisk double cream until stiff and put on top of meringue, leaving a 1 cm (½ in) gap around the edges. Prepare the fruit by washing it and removing any skin or stalks. Put on top of cream and meringue.

recipe idea
Try chocolate mousse instead of whipped cream and decorate with chocolate beans, grated chocolate and whipped cream.

recipe tips
Make sure the egg whites are at room temperature as this helps create a greater volume of meringue.
Egg whites will not whisk well unless the bowl is completely clean, dry and grease free.
Cook the meringue the night before you need it, leaving it to cool in the oven overnight.

sweet treats

sweet treats

- **makes:** 1 loaf - **preparation:** 45 minutes - **cooking:** 45 minutes
- **oven temperature:** 180°C (350°F/Gas mark 4)

apple crumble cake

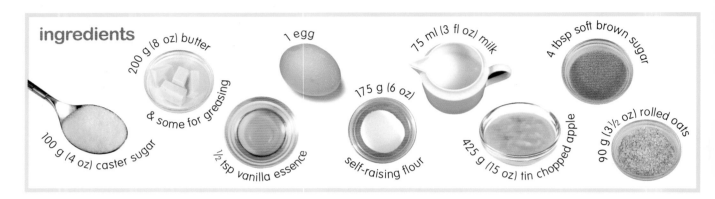

ingredients

200 g (8 oz) butter & some for greasing

1 egg

75 ml (3 fl oz) milk

4 tbsp soft brown sugar

100 g (4 oz) caster sugar

½ tsp vanilla essence

175 g (6 oz) self-raising flour

425 g (15 oz) tin chopped apple

90 g (3½ oz) rolled oats

1 Heat oven to 180ºC. Brush the loaf tin with oil/melted butter and line with greaseproof paper. Now regrease.

2 In a bowl, beat 100g (4oz) of the butter and sugar together until the mixture is pale and fluffy.

3 Break the egg into a small bowl and mix with a fork.

4 Gradually add egg to butter mixture, beating after each addition. Add vanilla essence.

5 Sift flour into bowl and fold in, gradually adding milk until ingredients are just combined.

You will also need greaseproof paper

9" x 5" x 3"

6 Put mixture into loaf tin, making sure top is level.

7 Open tin of chopped apple and put on top of cake mixture.

8 Put sugar, remaining butter and oats into a saucepan and stir until butter has melted.

9 Spoon crumble on top of cake. Bake for 45 minutes. Leave for 15 minutes to cool and remove from tin.

recipe tip
To remove cake from tin, place a cooling rack on top of cake tin and turn upside down. Remove tin and rest a plate on the cake. Hold cooling rack and plate with both hands and turn over.

sweet treats

- **makes:** 16 bars - **preparation:** 30 minutes - **cooking:** 50 minutes
- **oven temperature:** 170°C (325°F/Gas mark 3)

healthy energy bars

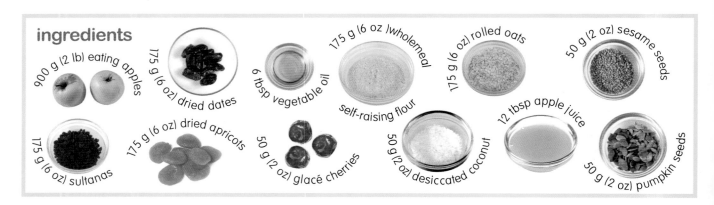

ingredients

900 g (2 lb) eating apples

175 g (6 oz) dried dates

6 tbsp vegetable oil

175 g (6 oz) wholemeal self-raising flour

175 g (6 oz) rolled oats

50 g (2 oz) sesame seeds

175 g (6 oz) sultanas

175 g (6 oz) dried apricots

50 g (2 oz) glacé cherries

50 g (2 oz) desiccated coconut

12 tbsp apple juice

50 g (2 oz) pumpkin seeds

1 Grease two 18 cm (7 in) square tins or baking trays or one large oblong. Preheat oven. Peel apples and finely chop. Put into saucepan with 1 tbsp water and cook slowly until all moisture has evaporated. Stir often with wooden spoon while cooking.

2 Chop dates and apricots. Put all remaining ingredients together in a bowl and mix well.

3 Put mixture into baking trays or tray and level with the back of a spoon.

4 Bake for 40 minutes on a low shelf. Move tray to top shelf for a further 10 minutes' cooking time. Cool until warm and cut into bars.

- **serves:** 8–10 - **preparation:** 30 minutes - **cooking:** 20 minutes
- **oven teperature:** 170°C (325°F/Gas mark 3)

sprinkle cake

ingredients

- 175 g (6 oz) self-raising flour
- 1 tsp baking powder
- 75 g (3 oz) multi-coloured sprinkles
- 3 eggs
- 175 g (6 oz) caster sugar
- 1 tsp vanilla essence
- 175 g (6 oz) margarine or butter

ingredients - Icing

- 175 g (6 oz) margarine or butter
- 1 tbsp milk
- 175 g (6 oz) icing sugar
- 1 tbsp cocoa powder
- 6 glacé cherries
- Extra multi-coloured sprinkles

1 Preheat oven. Grease two sandwich tins and line the bases with greaseproof paper.

2 Sift flour and baking powder into a mixing bowl. Add butter/margarine, caster sugar, eggs and vanilla essence.

3 Combine the mixture using wooden spoon or hand whisk.

4 Add multi-coloured sprinkles and fold in with a metal mixing spoon. Divide mixture evenly between sandwich tins. Bake in oven for 20 minutes and check to see if the cake is cooked. Leave to cool in the tins for 5 minutes, then turn out onto a wire cooling rack. Leave to cool completely.

5 To make icing, put butter, milk, icing sugar and cocoa powder into a clean bowl and whisk for several minutes until fluffy and well combined.

6 Peel greaseproof paper off cake bases. Put both cakes right way up and spread half of the icing onto each one, using a palette knife. Put one cake half on top of the other.

7 Gently rest a paper doily on top of the cake and sprinkle multi-coloured sprinkles over the holes in the doily. Carefully remove the doily and decorate cake with glacé cherries.

recipe idea
Make vanilla icing by substituting cocoa powder for ½ tsp vanilla essence. Spread a layer of jam on top of vanilla icing on bottom cake.

213

■ **serves:** 8–10 ■ **preparation:** 30 minutes ■ **cooking:** 1 hour
■ **oven temperature:** 190°C (375°F/Gas mark 5)

apricot tea loaf

ingredients

450 g (1 lb) dried apricots

450 ml (¾ pt) boiled water

350 g (12 oz) caster sugar

1 tsp salt

1 tsp ground cloves

2 eggs

175 g (6 oz) margarine/butter

½ tsp nutmeg

450 g (1 lb) plain flour

1 rounded tsp bicarbonate of soda

1 Preheat oven. Grease loaf tin with margarine.

2 Cut apricots into small pieces.

3 Place chopped apricots in a mixing bowl with boiled water, sugar, margarine/butter, spices and salt. Stir well and leave to stew for 5 minutes.

4 Break eggs into a cup and whisk with a fork. When the bowl of ingredients has cooled down, add the beaten eggs.

5 Sift flour and bicarbonate of soda into mixing bowl and fold in.

6 Pour mixture into prepared tin and bake for 1 hour. Check to see cake is cooked. Return cake to oven if it needs extra cooking.

7 When cooked, leave cake to cool for 5 minutes in the tin and then turn out onto a cooling rack.

sweet treats

■ **makes:** 8 mice ■ **preparation:** 30 minutes ■ **cooking:** 15 minutes
■ **oven temperature:** 190°C (375°F/Gas mark 5)

mice cakes

1 Preheat oven to 190°C. Line and grease Swiss roll tin and regrease the paper. In a mixing bowl, sieve the self-raising flour and baking powder. Add butter, caster sugar, eggs and vanilla essence.

ingredients

100 g (4 oz) self-raising flour

100 g (4 oz) butter/margarine

2 eggs

1 tsp baking powder

1 tsp vanilla essence

100 g (4 oz) caster sugar

Decoration

100 g (4 oz) butter

225 g (8 oz) icing sugar

1 tsp green food colouring

8 tinned pear halves, well drained

24 currants

16 chocolate buttons

4 strawberry laces

You will also need greaseproof paper

x2

12" x 8"

2 Beat with a wooden spoon/electric hand whisk until well combined. To check consistency, see page 26.

3 Spoon the mixture into Swiss roll tin and bake in the centre of the oven for 10–15 minutes until golden brown (to check cake is cooked, see page 26). Cool cake in tin for 2–3 minutes, then place cooling rack on top of tin and, holding tin and rack together (use oven gloves), turn upside down. Remove tin and greaseproof paper. Leave to cool.

4 Make the icing by beating butter, icing sugar and green food colouring together in a bowl. Add a little water if the icing is very stiff.

5 When cake is cool, trim the edges with a sharp knife to make sure they are straight. Spread the icing over the top of cake. Cut the cake into eight pieces (10 x 8 cm/4 x 3 in each).

6 Place a pear onto each cake. Push currants into 'nose' of each mouse to resemble eyes and nose. Make slits where the ears are and push chocolate buttons in carefully. Cut strawberry laces in half, make a small hole with the end of a knife and push ½ lace in to resemble a tail.

■ **serves:** 16–20 ■ **preparation:** 1 hour ■ **cooking:** 45 minutes
■ **oven temperature:** 190°C (375°F/Gas mark 5)

sweet treats

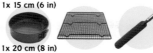

x2

1x 15 cm (6 in)

1x 20 cm (8 in)

You will also need greaseproof paper

You will also need a 40 cm (16 in) silver cake board

cat celebration cake

ingredients

275 g (10 oz) butter/margarine

275 g (10 oz) caster sugar

1 tsp baking powder

5 eggs

5 tbsp milk

Pinch of salt

275 g (10 oz) self-raising flour

decoration

60 g (2½ oz) butter

275 g (10 oz) icing sugar

1 tbsp cocoa powder

2 tbsp milk

Liquorice Allsorts and Liquorice laces

Few drops brown food colouring

chocolate matchsticks

1 Preheat oven. Grease two cake tins and line the bases with greaseproof paper.

2 Add butter and caster sugar to a mixing bowl and beat with a wooden spoon or whisk until pale and fluffy.

3 Break eggs into a cup and whisk with a fork. Gradually beat the eggs into the mixture.

4 Sift the flour, salt and baking powder into bowl and fold in with milk.

5 Divide mixture between the two tins, putting slightly more into the larger tin. With the back of a spoon, make a small dip in the centre of each tin. Bake small cake for 35 minutes and large cake for 45 minutes. Check the cakes are cooked. Turn each one out onto a wire cooling rack to cool completely.

6 To make the icing, mix butter, icing sugar, cocoa powder and milk in a clean mixing bowl. Beat with a wooden spoon until icing is smooth and fluffy. Add a few drops of brown food colouring and mix in. Add more colouring as needed to create the colour you want.

7 Rest the smaller cake over the edge of the bigger cake by 3 cm (1½ in).

8 Cut a curved slice into the larger cake. Cut the removed slice of cake in half to make two ears.

9 Put the large cake on the silver cake board and put the smaller cake into the cut-out curve to create the head and body of a cat. Place the ears at the top of the small cake in an appropriate position. Use a little icing to stick the pieces together.

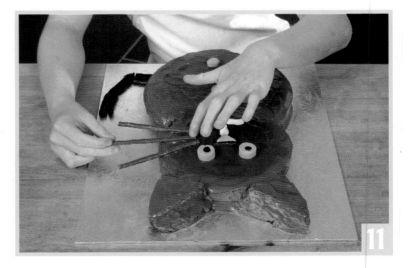

10 Use a palette knife to cover the entire cake with icing.

11 Use the sweets to make eyes, nose and some buttons. Use chocolate matchsticks for whiskers and liquorice laces for a mouth and tail.

drinks,
smoothies
& ices

homemade lemonade

1 Cut four lemons in half and squeeze the juice. Pour into large jug.

ingredients

Ice cubes

1 l (1 ¾ pt)
sparkling water

5 lemons

100 g (4 oz) sugar

2 Add sugar and sparkling water. Stir well.

3 Slice remaining lemon. Cut each slice in half and add to jug, along with approximately ten ice cubes. Serve in drinking glasses.

fruity punch

1 Squeeze out orange juice and add to large jug or bowl. Cut lemon and lime into slices and add to jug.

ingredients

4 oranges

½ lime

1 apple

½ lemon

8 cocktail cherries

2 tbsp sugar

500 ml (18 fl oz) apple juice

1 l (1 3/4 pt)

500 ml (18 fl oz) pineapple juice

lemonade

2 Cut apple into quarters and remove core. Slice apple.

3 Add to jug. Stir in sugar and cocktail cherries. Pour in fruit juices and lemonade. Stir well and serve.

banana & date smoothie

ingredients

2 bananas

6 dates (stones removed)

1 tsp honey

2 tbsp plain yogurt

300 ml (½ pt) milk

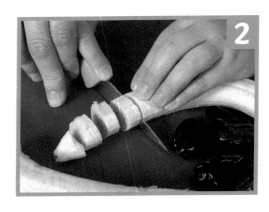

2

1 Peel the bananas.

2 Chop bananas into date-sized pieces.

3

4

3 Put all ingredients into jug.

4 Whizz until smooth.

recipe tip
Chopping ingredients to the same size makes a smoothie easier to blend.

mango & apricot smoothie

ingredients

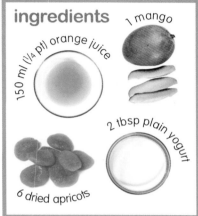

150 ml (¼ pt) orange juice

1 mango

2 tbsp plain yogurt

6 dried apricots

1 Peel and chop mango and put into jug.

2 Chop apricots and add to chopped mango.

recipe idea
Any tinned, fresh or dried fruit (and some vegetables) can be used in a smoothie, just remove skin and any stones or large pips. Try oranges, carrot, apple, strawberries, raspberries, blackcurrants, kiwi, peach, nectarine or pineapple. Flavoured yoghurt, fruit juices or ice cream can be added, even ice cubes or frozen fruits.

3 Add yogurt and orange juice and whizz until smooth.

fruit crush

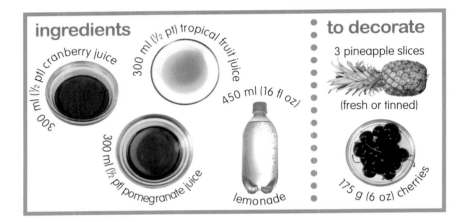

ingredients

300 ml (½ pt) cranberry juice

300 ml (½ pt) tropical fruit juice

300 ml (½ pt) pomegranate juice

450 ml (16 fl oz) lemonade

to decorate

3 pineapple slices (fresh or tinned)

175 g (6 oz) cherries

1 Pour pomegranate and cranberry juice into ice-cube trays and freeze until solid.

2 When ice cubes are frozen, mix tropical fruit juice and lemonade together in a large jug.

fruit kebabs

ingredients   ¼ melon

24 strawberries

1 Kiwi fruit

24 green seedless grapes

12 marshmallows

How to make it

Wash and dry strawberries and grapes. Remove strawberry stalks. Peel kiwi fruit and cut into quarters and then each quarter into three chunks. Peel skin from melon and cut into 12 chunks. Thread two strawberries, two grapes, a marshmallow and a chunk of kiwi and melon onto each wooden skewer.

milkshakes

ingredients

toffee banana milkshake

1 banana

300 ml (½ pt) milk

4 scoops toffee ice cream

strawberry milkshake

300 ml (½ pt) milk

100 g (4 oz) strawberries, stalks removed

4 scoops strawberry ice cream

summer-fruit shake

150 ml (¼ pt) milk

100 g (4 oz) raspberries, blackberries, strawberries

1 pot fruit yogurt

exotic shake

50 g (2 oz) pineapple slices

150 ml (¼ pt) coconut milk

1 peeled kiwi

or banana

150 ml (¼ pt) milk

Add ingredients for chosen milkshake to a jug and whizz until smooth. Serve immediately in a glass.

fruit ice lollies –
traffic-light ice lolly

ingredients

1 Kiwi fruit

4 dried apricots

4 strawberries

300 g (10½ oz) ready-made custard

1 Push one strawberry into bottom of each lolly mould. Place a dried apricot above the strawberry.

2 Peel and slice kiwi fruit. Put a slice of kiwi at top of mould and pour custard around fruit to fill each mould up. Freeze for 4 hours or overnight.

orange lolly

ingredients

1 large orange

350 ml (12 fl oz) pure orange juice

How to make it
Peel and slice an orange. Place 1–2 slices of orange into each lolly mould and top up with juice. Freeze for 4 hours or overnight.

strawberry & pineapple layer lolly

ingredients

225 ml (8 fl oz) pineapple juice

175 g (6 oz) strawberries

How to make it
Wash strawberries and remove stalks. Rest a sieve over a bowl and press strawberries through the sieve to purée strawberries and remove seeds. Divide strawberry purée between four lolly moulds and fill to top with pineapple juice. Freeze for 4 hours or overnight.

233

knickerbocker glory

ingredients

600 ml (1 pt) set strawberry jelly (make the day before)

2 bananas

4 small scoops vanilla ice cream

4 small scoops of strawberry ice cream

2 kiwis

sugar sprinkles to decorate

225 g (8 oz) strawberries

4 wafers

1 can ready-whipped cream

sauce

150 ml (¼ pt) double cream

175 g (6 oz) strawberries

2 tsp caster sugar

1 Place sauce ingredients in a bowl and, using hand blender, blend until everything is mixed together.

2 Wipe strawberries and remove the stalks, then slice. Peel kiwi fruit and slice. Peel bananas and also slice.

3 In each tall glass, spoon a layer of jelly and add a scoop of vanilla ice cream.

4 Divide fruit between glasses and drizzle two tablespoons of strawberry sauce into each glass.

recipe idea
Make a chocolate knickerbocker glory by using chocolate ice cream and making the sauce from 225 g (8 oz) chocolate, 300 ml (½ pt) double cream, 150 ml (¼ pt) water and 4 tsp caster sugar melted in a saucepan and stirred well.

5 Add a thin layer of jelly, followed by a scoop of strawberry ice cream. Top with more strawberry sauce and a wafer. Squirt whipped cream on top and decorate with sugar sprinkles. Serve with a long-handled spoon.

lemon cream sorbet

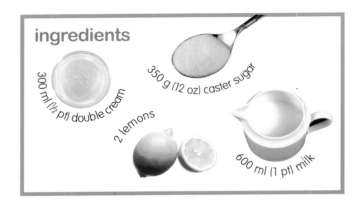

ingredients

300 ml (½ pt) double cream

350 g (12 oz) caster sugar

2 lemons

600 ml (1 pt) milk

1 Pour cream into mixing bowl and whisk until stiff and forming peaks when whisk is removed.

2 Grate rind from lemons, then cut lemons in half.

3 Squeeze juice from lemons. Stir juice and rind into whipped cream.

4 Add sugar and milk and stir until well combined. Pour mixture into a container and seal with a lid. Freeze until firm, approximately 2 hours.

5 Remove lid and cut sorbet into cubes. Pour chunks into a food processor and whizz until smooth and creamy. Alternatively, pour chunks back into a mixing bowl and use an electric hand whisk to blend ingredients.

6 Return the creamy mixture to container and freeze for a further 2 hours or until required.

recipe idea
To make orange cream sorbet, follow the same method, but add 175 ml (6 fl oz) of pure orange juice and the grated rind of 2 oranges in place of the lemon rind and juice.

index

acknowledgements

Firstly, thanks to David and Sarah for giving me the opportunity to write this book. Thanks also to my family and friends, who were my willing guinea pigs, and also to those who gave me extra recipe ideas and suggestions – you know who you are!

The children involved in cooking the recipes in this book were all fantastic fun to cook with and really well behaved. Hopefully you all enjoyed yourselves and learnt something, too.

Lastly, thanks to Chloe and Evie, my children, who gave up lots of their free time to test many recipes for me, not to mention attending many photo shoots.

The author and publishers would like to thank our special chefs for all their hard work:

Ben
Best food: candy floss & ice cream.
Worst food: carrots & celery.

Georgia
Best food: chocolate & sweeties.
Worst food: tomatoes.

Chloe
Best food: spaghetti bolognaise.
Worst food: my school-dinner chips.

Evie
Best food: sausage & chips.
Worst food: tomato ketchup.

Ben
Best food: lettuce.
Worst food: tomatoes.

Alex
Best food: pasties.
Worst food: pancakes.

Nicholas
Best food: chips.
Worst food: beefburgers.

Sammi
Best food: chocolate.
Worst food: hot chilli.

Yara
Best food: ham.
Worst food: mushrooms.

Jamie
Best food: carrots.
Worst food: tomatoes.

Alison
Best food: chocolate.
Worst food: cabbage.

Alex
Best food: pizza.
Worst food: broccoli.

Megan
Best food: strawberries.
Worst food: custard.

Molly
Best food: roast dinner.
Worst food: sweets.

Kit
Best food: pasta.
Worst food: peppers.